PARALLEL PLAY

PARALLEL PLAY

Growing Up with
Undiagnosed Asperger's

Tim Page

DOUBLEDAY
New York   London   Toronto
Sydney   Auckland

Ⅽⅅ

DOUBLEDAY

www.doubleday.com

DOUBLEDAY and the DD colophon are registered trademarks
of Random House, Inc.

Portions of *Parallel Play* were originally published in
The New Yorker.

Grateful acknowledgment is made to the following for
permission to reproduce their photographs:
Chapter Nine: From the personal photo collection of
John A. Carini.
Acknowledgments: Photo by Christina Clarke.

Book design by Michael Collica

Library of Congress Cataloging-in-Publication Data
Page, Tim, 1954–
Parallel play : growing up with undiagnosed Asperger's / by
Tim Page. — 1st ed.
p. cm.
1. Page, Tim, 1954– —Childhood and youth. 2. Asperger's
syndrome—Patients—Biography. 3. Music critics—United
States—Biography. I. Title.
RC553.A88P34 2009
362.196'8588320092—dc22
[B]
2009003595

ISBN 978-0-385-52562-6

PRINTED IN THE UNITED STATES OF AMERICA

1 3 5 7 9 10 8 6 4 2

First Edition

For my sons, William, Robert, and John, with the hope that this book may explain some things—and for Philip Glass, with affection and gratitude.

Be kind, for everyone you meet is fighting a
great battle.

—Anonymous, often attributed
to Philo of Alexandria

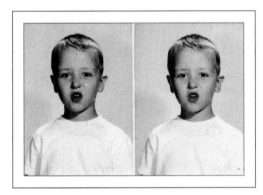

Kindergarten class photo, Ypsilanti, Michigan. Try
as I might, I couldn't remember how to smile.

My second-grade teacher never liked me much, and one assignment I turned in annoyed her so extravagantly that the red pencil with which she scrawled "See me!" broke through the lined paper. Our class had been asked to write about a recent field trip, and, as was so often the case in those days, I had noticed the wrong things:

> Well, we went to Boston, Massachusetts
> through the town of Warrenville, Connecticut
> on Route 44A. It was very pretty and there was
> a church that reminded me of pictures of
> Russia from our book that is published by

Time-Life. We arrived in Boston at 9:17. At 11
we went on a big tour of Boston on Gray Line
43, made by the Superior Bus Company like
School Bus Six, which goes down Hunting
Lodge Road where Maria lives and then on to
Separatist Road and then to South Eagleville
before it comes to our school. We saw lots of
good things like the Boston Massacre site. The
tour ended at 1:05. Before I knew it we were
going home. We went through Warrenville
again but it was too dark to see much. A few
days later it was Easter. We got a cuckoo clock.

It is an unconventional but hardly unobservant report.
In truth, I cared not one bit about Boston on that windy
spring day in 1963. Instead, I wanted to learn about Warrenville, a village a few miles northeast of the township of
Mansfield, Connecticut, where my family was then living. I
had memorized the map of Mansfield—available for one
dollar from our municipal office—and knew all the school-
bus routes by heart, a litany I sang out to anybody I could
corner. But Warrenville was in the township of Ashford, for
which I had no guide, and I remember my blissful sense of
resolution when I verified that Route 44A crossed Route 89
in the town center, for I had long hypothesized that they
might meet there. Of such joys and pains was my childhood
composed.

I received a grade of "Unsatisfactory" in Social Development from the Mansfield Public Schools that year. I did not
work to the best of my ability, did not show neatness and

care in assignments, did not cooperate with the group, and did not exercise self-control. About the only positive assessment was that I worked well independently. Of course. Then as now, it was all that I could do.

In the years since the phrase became a cliché, I have received any number of compliments for my supposed ability to "think outside the box." Actually, it has been a struggle for me to perceive just what these "boxes" were— why they were there, why other people regarded them as important, where their borderlines might be, how to live safely within and without them. My efforts have only partly succeeded; at the age of fifty-three, I am left with the melancholy sensation that my life has been spent in a perpetual state of parallel play, alongside, but distinctly apart from, the rest of humanity.

From early childhood, my memory was so acute and my wit so bleak that I was described as a genius—by my parents, by neighbors, and even, on occasion, by the same teachers who handed me failing marks. I wrapped myself in this mantle, of course, as a poetic justification for behavior that might otherwise have been judged unhinged, and I did my best to believe in it. But the explanation made no sense. A genius at *what*? Were other "geniuses" so oblivious that they needed mnemonic devices to tell right from left, and idly wet their pants into adolescence? What accounted for my rages and frustrations, for the imperious contempt I showed to people who were in a position to do me harm? Although I delighted in younger children, whom I could instruct and gently dominate, and exulted when I ran across an adult who was willing to discuss my pet subjects,

I could establish no connection with most of my classmates. My pervasive childhood memory is an excruciating awareness of my own strangeness.

And so, between the ages of seven and fifteen, I was given glucose-tolerance tests, anti-seizure medications, electro-encephalograms, and an occasional Mogadon tablet to shut me down at night. I suffered through a summer of Bible camp; exercise regimens were begun and abandoned; the school brought in its own psychiatrist to grill me once a week. Somehow, every June, I was promoted to the next grade, having accomplished little to deserve it. Meanwhile, the more kindly teachers, recognizing that I would be tormented on the playground, permitted me to spend recess periods indoors, where I memorized vast portions of the 1961 edition of the *World Book Encyclopedia* simply by skimming through its volumes.

A brown carton in my basement contains most of the surviving documents of my elementary-school years, and they present a pretty fair portrait of my preteen obsessions. There are intricately detailed street maps of make-believe cities on which I worked silently for hours; countless crayon drawings of grinning girls with shoulder-length hair and U-shaped smiles, their stick figures fleshed out only by exaggerated biceps; obituaries of Sophie Tucker, Edward R. Murrow, and David O. Selznick torn from the *Hartford Courant* and pasted sloppily into a scrapbook; any number of meandering and implausible stories, none of them with happy endings.

In my darker moods, I think that the rest of my life can be quickly summarized: I grew up and into other preoccupations, some of which served me well, without ever managing to admit the full tide of human experience.

I was told that I had Asperger's syndrome in the fall of 2000, as part of what had become a protracted effort to identify—and, if possible, alleviate—my lifelong unease. I had never heard of the condition, which had been recognized by the American Psychiatric Association only six years earlier. Nevertheless, the diagnosis was one of those rare clinical confirmations met mostly with relief. Here, finally, was an objective explanation for some of my strengths and weaknesses, the simultaneous capacity for unbroken work and all-encompassing recall, linked inextricably to a driven, uncomfortable personality. And I learned that there were others like me—people who yearned for steady routines, repeated patterns, and a few cherished subjects, the driftwood that keeps us afloat.

The syndrome was identified, in 1944, by Hans Asperger, a Viennese pediatrician, who wrote, "For success in science or art, a dash of autism is essential." In *Asperger's Syndrome: A Guide for Parents and Professionals,* Tony Attwood observed, "The person with Asperger's syndrome has no distinguishing physical features but is primarily viewed by other people as different because of their unusual quality of social behavior and conversation skills. For example, a woman with Asperger's syndrome described how as a child she saw people moving into the house up the street, ran up to one of the new kids and, instead of the conventional greeting and request of 'Hi, you want to play?,' proclaimed, 'Nine times nine is equal to 81.' "

David Mamet, in his book *Bambi vs. Godzilla,* discerned

redeeming qualities in the condition. Considering film-makers past and present, he stated that "it is not impossible that Asperger's syndrome helped make the movies. The symptoms of this developmental disorder include early precocity, a great ability to maintain masses of information, a lack of ability to mix with groups in age-appropriate ways, ignorance of or indifference to social norms, high intelligence, and difficulty with transitions, married to a preternatural ability to concentrate on the minutia of the task at hand."

The Asperger's spectrum ranges from people barely more abstracted than a stereotypical "absent-minded professor" to the full-blown, albeit highly functioning, autistic. Symptoms of Asperger's have been attributed ex post facto to renowned and successful individuals, but these are the fortunate ones—persons able to invent outlets for their ever-cresting monomanias. Many are not so lucky, and end up institutionalized, homeless, or merely miserable and alone. And yet for some—record collectors with every catalog number at hand, theater buffs with first-night casts memorized, children who draw precise architectural blueprints of nineteenth-century silk mills—a cluster of facts can be both luminous and lyric, something around which to construct a life.

We are informally referred to as "Aspies," and if we are not very, very good at something we tend to do it very poorly. Little comes naturally—except for whatever random, inexplicable, and often uncontrollable gifts we may have—and, even more than most children, we assemble our personalities unevenly, in bits and pieces, almost robotically, from models we admire. (I remember the deliberate decision to appropriate one teacher's mischievous grin and darting eyes, which I found so charming that I thought they might work for me, too.) A lot of Aspies share certain interests—film, music, electronics, maps, mathematics, history—and we tend to get along instantly if those interests coincide. Yet we are not always natural companions; if, say, you introduce an Aspie devotee of antique piano recordings to one whose passion is vacuum cleaners, chances are that the meeting will result in two uncomprehending and increasingly agitated monologues.

So preoccupied are we with our inner imperatives that the outer world may overwhelm and confuse. What anguished pity I used to feel for piñatas at birthday parties, those papier-mâché donkeys with their amiable smiles about to be shattered by little brutes with bats! On at least one occasion, I begged for a stay of execution and eventually had to be taken home, hysterical, convinced that I had just witnessed the braining of a new and sympathetic acquaintance.

Caring for inanimate objects came easily. Learning to make connections with people—much as I desperately wanted to—was a bewildering process, for they kept *changing*, and I felt like an alien, always about to be exposed. Or, to adapt another hoary but useful analogy, not only did I not see the forest for the trees; I was so intensely distracted that I missed the trees for the species of lichen on their bark.

The author and neurologist Oliver Sacks distinguishes between full-fledged autism and Asperger's syndrome. In *The New Yorker* some years ago, Sacks wrote that "people with Asperger's syndrome can tell us of their experiences, their inner feelings and states, whereas those with classical autism cannot. With classical autism there is no 'window,' and we can only infer. With Asperger's syndrome there is self-consciousness and at least some power to introspect and report."

And so what follows—the story of my childhood—may be counted as one person's attempt to open a "window," and I will do my best to keep the report as honest as I can. This necessarily includes the fact that I was a glum little atheist at a precocious age, who would only later discern spiritual traces in music, books, films, good company, and an occasional October afternoon. But I can't soften what I felt at the time, for telling the truth about my life seems to me not only the moral imperative of this book but its sole excuse. I'm not going to put undue stress on my Asperger's syndrome; it will be there, but not front and center, in part because that was only one element of what made me, and in part because I had no idea what it was until I was forty-five. Nor do I possess the qualifications to write one of those "how to cope" books: I wish I had some universal wisdom to impart to readers with Asperger's but I'm still struggling myself, and I expect my struggle to continue until the day I die. All I can offer is a personal chronicle—and sometimes it will be very personal indeed, to a degree that I would have found unbearable when I was younger. So be it: I am now in my mid-fifties, far closer to the end than to the beginning, and I can only be embarrassed for so long.

ONE

Commanding the record player at 3650 Alcott
Street, San Diego, March 1958.

My memories begin in a fragrant California backyard,
when I was two years old. The yard remains, infinitely
smaller than it once seemed but still heady with eucalyptus
oil and sudden gusts of ocean air, just as it was in 1956. We
lived at 3650 Alcott Street, high above Point Loma, in a
small subdivision of what had been the ornate formal gar-
dens of the Appleton Bridges estate, and the leftover elegance—rows of fruit trees, a stone birdbath, the intricate
latticework on the patio, and the dry bed of a decorative
brook—is virtually unchanged, as is the continual thunder
of planes descending into San Diego International Airport
a few hundred feet away. On a cool summer evening, it is

easy to imagine my mother and father stepping out of our silent, grainy home movies and back into vibrant life. From the balcony they wave to me, a red-cheeked boy in a blue romper, squinting up into the sunset and stumbling merrily behind my paternal grandmother, always known as Gaga, as she waters the parsley and avocado.

I was happy there, in this balmy Eden preserved dimly in scent and sensation. Everything seemed eternal; I felt loved and protected and sure that this would continue forever. What comfort I found in normality, in a world where nothing ever happened! My days were a series of unbroken routines: the friendly mailman with jingling pockets who arrived in late morning; the constitutional walk around the block (a spotted cat usually stretched herself sleepily in a picture window on Alcott Street); and then, as I already found naps impossible, an hour or two with the phonograph records my mother had tacitly agreed to let me ruin by playing them over and over, lifting and dropping the big brown tonearm with my tiny, clumsy hands.

Watching the records spin, I was astonished at their evocation of aural worlds that I not only instinctively understood but in which I actually felt at home. Music moved at three speeds then: the long-playing albums that turned 33⅓ times a minute, the faster 45s that required a special spindle in their centers, and the heavy old 78s that shattered so easily and that nobody seemed to care about much anymore. I was emperor of them all, and thought I divined everything their sounds had to convey—whether it was a detailed story ("Here's the part where the dog bites the man," I explained to my father) or merely the perfect, wordless definition of a germinal feeling. I was especially drawn to music that was nearly changeless, unfolding slowly and inevitably, with few surprises—Ravel's *Bolero,* the "Carol of the Bells," and the "Sunrise" movement from Ferde Grofé's *Grand Canyon Suite,* which fixed me in a state of steady ecstasy, as though I were caught up in the very process of life.

But then, late on a Sunday afternoon just before my third birthday, all was spoiled. My grandfather Frank Homer Page, whose stomach had hurt for as long as I'd known him, simply vanished, and nobody would give me a satisfactory explanation for where he had gone. By nighttime, his bed was neatly made up, with an eerie and unprecedented tidiness that somehow suggested that the covers would not be disturbed for a long time. I was ushered out of the room and, through somebody's tears, told that Granddaddy was in heaven now and that I should be glad. I was not.

A week or two later, I was brought to Fort Rosecrans National Cemetery and expected to reconcile my grandfather's mysterious new home above the world with the patch of ground beneath which, somehow, he also dwelt. The graveyard, a federal landmark set out on a breezy peninsula surrounded by ocean, was brilliantly sunny that day, a more convincing paradise than the bleached realm of puffed clouds and baby blond angels that had been displayed to me in a book back home. Still, something unreal and sinister was going on, and I resented it. Gaga was definitely crying; so, perhaps, was my father, and I was not permitted to run up or roll down the Fort Rosecrans hill despite its irresistibly inviting slopes. There were fixed smiles all around, but nobody was happy and, although it would be years before I knew how to express it, I felt that my intelligence had been insulted mightily.

Thereafter, my grandfather, who had always treated me so tenderly, became frightening in his absence and soon I was afraid to summon his visual image. I avoided his photographs and he lingered on only as the memory of a perennially welcoming lap amid a bathrobe full of bones, as a tired voice from the next room, as the remnant of sharp but curiously consoling stubble that had brushed against my cheek when he stooped down to kiss me. His unfathomable but intensely felt gone-ness chilled me, and I was certain only that someone else would depart soon, and just as suddenly.

My parents made me pray before bedtime, but I now mistrusted God and had no patience for religious comfort. Instead, I wanted definite answers to specific questions, and I devised a nightly catechism for my mother, one that had to be said in precisely the same order, with the same responses, or we would have to start over again: "Will you die tonight? Will Dad? Will there be a wild boar? Will a saber-toothed tiger come back to life and eat me?" Once, in the middle of Southern California's brief, fierce rainy season, my mother had the happy inspiration to assure me that the house couldn't burn that night because the whole city had been drenched in a storm. This calmed me for the moment but had the unanticipated side effect of raising future expectations. Thereafter, I included a new query in my litany;

I refused to sleep before I had been promised not only that there wouldn't be a fire but that it was too wet for one.

The quotations from her oldest child which my mother preserved in her diary may have sounded cute at the time, but they now strike me as unremittingly desolate. "Someday will it never be a day again?" was one recurring, Gertrude Stein-ian koan. Or, following a visit to the cemetery: "Where is heaven? When will I go? How will I get there? What does God look like? Does Granddaddy's stomach still hurt? Will you wait for me if you go first?" And then this entry from February 25, 1959: "Tonight, after his prayer, Timmy said, 'God, please don't let me die. God isn't good to let us die, is he?' "

"Tim's going to fight this thing!" my mother wrote, decorating her sentiment with a little smiley face, long before the symbol became ubiquitous. She was right, and the battle consumed much of my energy. There came a time when the cat in the Alcott Street window disappeared—for a day, then a week, then forever. My mother couldn't explain what had happened—the family didn't seem to have moved away—and so a fresh anxiety tinged our walks. Even my record-playing was affected: when I was told that Jean Sibelius had recently died, *Finlandia* took on an otherworldly grandeur. It suddenly became death music, a message from beyond, perhaps from the place where my grandfather lived. Arthur Rubinstein's recording of Manuel de Falla's *Ritual Fire Dance* had always spooked me—its furious, thrusting trills conjured up images of an attack of bees. However, with the news that de Falla, too, had just died (and how *did* I learn these things?) my exuberant, roller-coaster sort of fun fear was supplanted by a gut terror so intense that I could no longer bear to have the record played. Even my father's pop albums triggered dark ruminations; one night, captivated by the close harmonies of a celebrated singing group, I wondered gloomily whether the Four Freshmen knew that we were alive.

Gaga was the person who convinced me that every living thing would die, but, in fairness to her kind heart, I gave her no choice in the matter. We had been talking about her brother Franklin, who had succumbed to scarlet fever when he was eighteen months old, his scrap of existence preserved only in a single photograph, a pleasant-faced child, scarcely begun and seemingly much too sweetly ordinary to have suffered such a fate. But, yes, Franklin had been taken to heaven, Gaga explained with distant sorrow, and I realized with a start that he had been even younger than I was. This opened the door to all sorts of uncomfortable questions, which my grandmother dutifully answered as lovingly as she could, but with the firm, no-nonsense resolve of a minister's daughter whose faith was not of the Earth. After a while, there was no mistaking her meaning: although it probably wouldn't happen for a long, long time, I, too, was doomed.

I argued with her, doing my best to change her mind, make her admit that she was wrong, or confess that it was all a joke. I'd pretend to drop the subject and we'd speak of other things, but I always circled back to the big question, with the crafty insistence of a miniature trial lawyer intent on breaking a key witness. She remained immovable, however, and finally I believed her, at least for a moment, and I ran out into the sun-blanched yard, howling louder than the planes, newly aware of my body and its awful impermanence, from which I could not escape, no matter where I went, no matter what I did.

Somebody told my father and when he came home he tried to help, with a sort of existential commiseration that I wouldn't necessarily recommend to parents of distressed four-year-olds. His answer was to read to me—in a deep, richly cadenced voice that gave me my first glimmering that words could be as eloquent as music—but it was all poetry of loss and mourning: "The Rubaiyat of Omar Khayyam," *A Shropshire Lad,* and T. S. Eliot. One line from "East Coker" was especially worrisome:

Oh dark dark dark. They all go into the dark.

My father and mother, Ellis Batten Page and Elizabeth Latimer Thaxton Page, were then in their mid-thirties. My mother was elegant and gentle, temperamentally reserved but infinitely openhearted, and unwavering in her conviction that any setbacks her children faced could be overcome. I adored her. Once, as she was bathing me, we decided to figure out how old we would be when the new century and the new millennium arrived in the year 2000. I would be forty-six that year, we decided—or, to put it more exactly (as I'm sure I would have insisted upon doing even then), I would *turn* forty-six and she would *turn* seventy-six. We agreed to wait for each other and, in sentimental moods, I like to imagine that she deliberately honored her vow, as she fought off her final illness until the early morning of January 16, 2000.

My relationship with my father was more complicated, and I feel his presence in the room as I type these words, although he, too, has been dead for years. The books in our house mostly belonged to him, and while I understood my mother's records instinctively, with no need for outside interpretation, I had to ask my father just what was in the hundreds of volumes on his shelves, as I was still learning to read. And so he told me about Ernest Hemingway and F. Scott Fitzgerald and Thomas Wolfe, his favorite almost-contemporary writers, read me passages from their works, and let me stay up to watch *The Old Man and the Sea* with him on television. On my own, I shuddered through *Modern Mexican Art,* published by the University of Minnesota Press in 1939 and filled with terrifying images: hanged men, peasant women overladen with dead chickens, parents weeping over what I hoped were only sleeping children. Even the Sun God looked bloodthirsty.

Through my father, I gleaned that books were magical and later on I would sometimes close whatever volume I was reading—*The Story of Ferdinand, Half Magic, Goodbye, Mr. Chips*—and hold it out in front of me, close to tears, marveling at its riches and wondering whether I might someday create something comparable. My father introduced me to one published author, an old friend named Leonard Huish, and told me discreetly vague stories of yet another, William S. Burroughs, whom he had come to know and to disapprove of during the course of a bohemian year in Mexico City. But the first writer I knew well was my grandmother's tenant, Alan M. Kriegsman, who, with his wife, Sali Ann, moved into the main house after my grandfather died, while Gaga had a small apartment constructed for herself on the property. Mike, as he was called by everyone but his casual readers, was then the music critic for the *San Diego Union.* He played his Steinway grand with what seemed to me breathtaking finesse. I can still recall his rendition of Chopin's second étude, the tiny finger twister in A minor, which struck me as an uncanny musical depiction of a spider rapidly crawling up and down a web.

Almost every night Mike attended a concert, wrote it up, and we could read all about it in the morning paper. I could imagine no better way to live. More than thirty-five years later, we would work together as critics some 2,600 miles away at the *Washington Post* (indeed, we would both win Pulitzer prizes there), which seems an extraordinary coincidence. But of course it was not altogether coincidental; Mike was one of my first heroes, and his example granted me permission, at an early and impressionable age, to think and write independently about music. Never for a moment thereafter did I want to be a fireman, a policeman, a movie star, or even the president—none of the usual fantasy futures for young American boys. No, I wanted to read and think and listen to music, and Mike made it clear that such a life was possible.

I was lucky that I was an early reader, for insomnia had become a problem by the time I was four (almost all the voracious readers I've known have had difficulty sleeping). From everything I've heard, San Diego was a beautiful but rather dull place in the 1950s, although as a port city it must have had a robust underground life that few discussed at the time. Still, after my grandfather died, the mild Southern California nights terrified me—our house shaded by a dead man who was said to be both beneath the soil and above the clouds but nevertheless found time to watch over us all the time, whether we wanted him to or not. The deep blue skies were occasionally parted by sweeping, disruptive searchlights that I did not understand but knew that I did not like, and somewhere nearby there was an experimental wind tunnel that made a hollow, eerie *whoosh* that sounded as though an angry giant were blowing across the top of a huge empty bottle.

Occasionally, my mother would let me spend some of the night with her; more typically, I had to content myself with Mario, Brownie, Charcoal, Hexie, or one of the other stuffed animals who were my best friends, endowed with their own distinct personalities, and the only toys I willingly accepted as gifts in lieu of books or records. Of these, Mario, a floppy white dog with brown ears that I named for the inspired and unruly tenor Mario Lanza, was my favorite and I would hold on to him tightly until I forgot myself into sleep. Mario remained my bedmate up to my late teens, at which point I cast him out with embarrassment and he was replaced by more vibrant and complicated (if less reliably reassuring) companions, whenever they could be found. He was a sure and steadfast comfort, and I would not be surprised if I called for Mario on my deathbed.

Throughout the late fifties and early sixties, Walter Cronkite was the host of a weekly documentary television series called *Twentieth Century,* which showed a great deal of footage from World War II, and I noticed that the TV sound of a falling bomb closely resembled that of a plane coming in for a landing, something that happened directly above our heads hundreds of times a day. And so, late into the night, as another plane began its approach, I played a grim, fraught little guessing game with myself: was I listening to the arrival of a routine TWA or Pan Am flight into San Diego, or were the Russians finally dropping the bomb on us? Usually I was able to convince myself that it was only an airplane—only an *airplane,* ONLY AN AIRPLANE!!!—but then the roar would intensify, to an ever-more-deafening volume, pummeling the windows and rattling the china, and I would have no doubt that my little life was over.

An apocalyptic bent was not uncommon in those days, nor was it unfounded. Nikita Khrushchev was a recurring figure in my nightmares. Decades later, a friend would take me to dinner with Robert McNamara, the secretary of defense in the Kennedy and Johnson administrations. The film *Thirteen Days,* about the Cuban Missile Crisis, which came close to setting off nuclear war between the United States and the Soviet Union, had just been released, and I asked McNamara whether things had really been as dangerous as they had been portrayed onscreen. "Infinitely more dangerous," he replied quietly. "I know things now that I didn't know then, and I'm amazed we survived."

My own memory of the Missile Crisis is of splashing aimlessly in a bathtub while my parents watched Kennedy's speech on television in the next room. My father came in and sat by me, his face pained and his voice halting. "Tim, we're going to have to blockade Cuba," he said, and I had no idea what he meant. But there was no mistaking his next statement: "It looks like the beginning of World War III." And the water turned to ice around my scrotum.

One more image from those years, after the family had moved to Connecticut. It must have been early June, back when summers seemed eternal and our Norway maples were in their fullest dark-green glory. My father and I had both been reading in the yard—our relationship was always smoothest when conducted on an intellectual basis—and I noticed that he had put his book down and was watching me intently. "Enjoy your life, old Timmer," he said, his heart in every word. "There may not be as much of it as there should be." And he went on to explain that our new home lay between New York and Boston, two cities that would certainly be bombed if we went to war, with our university town caught in the resulting firestorm.

Someday it would never be a day again.

Throughout the 1960s, my father was constantly drawing up and abandoning plans to build a bomb shelter under our house. I loved the idea at the outset—a cool new hideout where we could play with the kids across the street! But no, my father insisted gravely, we couldn't tell Nicky and Lulu, because if the bomb dropped and they came over we'd have to protect ourselves and might have to shoot them. And I had a horrid prefiguration of blond, cute-as-a-button three-year-old Lulu morphing with Faye Dunaway in *Bonnie and Clyde,* bouncing around bloodily in her white party dress as dozens of machine-gun bullets blasted her body apart.

This was a time when children knew that death could come from the sky at any moment—an appalling recognition—but it was also the period of the ambitious NASA programs that would ultimately lead to moon landings. On launch mornings, our teachers would dispatch us from class to lug our chairs down to the gymnasium, where a black-and-white television set had been placed on top of a ladder for us to watch history as it happened. The countdown was exhilarating—"Ten! Nine! Eight!" we shouted along as lustily as possible—and then all was fire, smoke, propulsion, and wrenching motion as the rocket lifted off. After a time, the first stage would fall away, and then the second, until there was only a tiny capsule moving through the darkness. By then, I was solemn. That's me, I thought—alone, unsupported, and hurtling through space, on my way toward nothingness.

My younger sister and brother experienced no such alienation. On the contrary, they were content and well-adjusted, and I couldn't quite figure them out. With each new arrival, the dynamics in our house changed utterly, and I was especially jealous of Betsy, who had been born about twenty months after I was. Once, when I was about two, I was caught throwing handfuls of sand and dirt on her as she screamed in her baby carriage. I envied our pediatrician his privilege of sticking needles into the unwanted intruder and making her cry, something that I knew would have got me into serious trouble. "Timmy continually uses violent language," my mother noted in her diary. "This afternoon he got very angry and came up with a real prize: 'Betsy, I'm going to smash your little bones!' " But I loved my brother, Rick, pretty much from the start. At three and a half, I was just old enough to be enchanted by the soft, glowing peace of a sleeping baby, and he was a beauty. I called him Ricky Dandelion, a nickname that, fortunately for my brother, never stuck.

And so our family of five was completed. It was obvious early on that I was going to be strange, and that Betsy, with her inborn steadiness, intelligence, and sociability, would succeed at whatever she pursued. But Rick's fate was more specific—he was a born doctor. I doubt that he ever gave any other reply to that question so beloved of grown-ups: "What do you want to be when you grow up?" He progressed cheerfully and inevitably from toy black bags and little white coats through microscopes, med school, and beyond.

Every night before dinner, we would participate in a ritual invented by my father, which was originally dubbed Loving Family Group and eventually shortened to LFG. After sitting down at the table, we held hands and recited, in chant rhythm: "We are a loving family group—one for all and all for one." Then we'd say our own personal prayers before finishing off with a traditional "God is great; God is good; let us thank Him for our food. Amen." At that point, we were free to eat.

I had nothing against LFG, except on those days when I had quarreled with somebody in the family and would snarl "One for all and all for one" through clenched teeth. But the interpolated prayer presented problems, for its purpose eluded me. I had figured out that asking for a specific present or hoping that I wouldn't get beat up at the bus stop were both insufficiently metaphysical. Nor was it considered polite to wish for the death of a teacher. So I usually grumbled something along the lines of "Thank you" and gazed down into my casserole.

A petitionary prayer was also required when we entered our pew at church, where I spent some of the least spiritual hours of my childhood. There, week after week, I would kneel as devoutly as I could, bow my head, and express the identical silent yearning: *"Please* let this end soon." Later incarceration in a Baptist camp throughout the roast hot summer of 1966—that edgy, transformative season of the back-to-back massacres of Richard Speck and Charles Whitman, riots in Cleveland, Atlanta, and San Francisco, "King of the Road" blasting from every radio—did nothing to increase my reverence.

Indeed, the only time I can remember praying with any urgency was on the morning of March 18, 1960, when our parents roused us with a tearful command to fall to our knees. We were then in Ypsilanti, Michigan, during a nomadic period when my father moved from campus to campus, climbing the academic ladder. Three houses up the street lived my first true friend, Amy Callahan, with whom I used to walk to Roosevelt Elementary School a few blocks away. She was an absolute master of the paths and hiding places in the undeveloped woods near Washtenaw Avenue, which I had been forbidden to cross, something I never admitted to Amy as I followed her along, marveling at her daring and her agility. My father had gleaned that I thought her very special and used to tease me by crooning a Frank Loesser song called "Once in Love with Amy," which made me blush. The Page and Callahan doors were never locked during the daytime, so we went in and out of each other's houses constantly, without bothering to knock or ring.

That was all over now. After Betsy and I had been kneeling by the bedside for a few moments, hearts pounding like timpani, wondering what could possibly have happened, my father summoned the strength to report the awful news. Amy's mother, Mary Jean Callahan, someone we saw every day and loved for her perpetually warm welcomes, had fallen asleep with a cigarette in hand and set her chair—and then herself—on fire. Thanks to a neighbor's insistence, a member of the rescue team had found Amy sleeping upstairs and carried her to safety.

We sobbed for a while, and Betsy vowed on the spot that she would never smoke a cigarette. It was a slate-gray Michigan morning, dusky snow covered the ground all over Fairview Circle, and the firemen had placed what was left of Mrs. Callahan's red overstuffed chair, a ghastly public souvenir, in front of Amy's charred white house. As we drove by, I fell uncharacteristically silent; when my mother inquired, I explained that I was "trying to push the sadness out of my heart."

I'm proud to say that my friendship with Amy persists to this day, and she recently shared with me a letter that my father sent to her family after the fire:

The fact that continues to reverberate as I think about [Mary Callahan] is that we never heard her say an unkind thing to or about a living creature. She was a wonderful neighbor, helpful when help was needed, gracious and generous. The impact which these qualities had already had on the children I believe were strong and deep. We thought she was a wonderful mother: she *is* a wonderful mother. Her shocking and sudden death will in no way erase the imprint of her loving and lovable personality on those two adorable girls. In this sense her immortality is assured.

Throughout his life, my father found it easier to convey deep feeling in carefully crafted written words than in any sort of spontaneous verbal expression. Some twenty years later, it would be my discovery of a letter he wrote defending me against the slanders of a school administrator—a letter I was unaware of at the time, when I genuinely thought my father had taken the other side—that ended a long estrangement. Since then, and especially since his death, I have come to see him as a person of innate natural tenderness, a quality insufficiently valued in men of his generation, that was further slapped out of him by the privations of the Great Depression, the stoicism of the Marine Corps code (he fought in the last days of World War II), and the general public veneration, shared by my father, of Ernest Hemingway's huntin' and shootin' literary persona, described by Max Eastman as "false hair on the chest."

My father regarded me as companionable in part because I was the only one in the family with whom he could share his dread, my mother being much too occupied with the pressing duties of raising small children. And so, while waiting for the apocalypse, he suggested stories for me to read—J. D. Salinger's "Teddy," Katherine Mansfield's "Life of Ma Parker," O. Henry's "Gift of the Magi"—and he took me to films. The French short *The Red Balloon* was a favorite, although even at the age of five the budding critic in me found the fantasy ending impossibly roseate and my instinct would have been to leave poor Pascal sitting disconsolately by the broken body of his ruined friend as the mob laughed and jeered and the credits came up—death *without* transfiguration.

And Ingmar Bergman's *Wild Strawberries* had a profound effect on me, even though I could barely read the English subtitles, which were white-on-white for much of the film. But I was mesmerized by the image of the gentle old man, already half in the grave and surrounded by ghosts, searching through his past for fragments of meaning and fulfillment before it is all over. I missed many of the nuances, but I entered its dream world immediately and intuitively, and it strikes me now that I am emulating Bergman's Isak Borg, sifting through my own life to create this testament.

TWO

With Brownie, Mario, and Charcoal in
Denton, Texas, early 1961.

When I was forty-two, in the summer after my mother
lost her reason, I moved into the family home for a few
weeks to look after my damaged, disoriented father, so suddenly aged, and to sort through the boxes of family papers
that he had repeatedly threatened, as if a necessary purga-
tion, to throw out at any time.

My mother had saved everything—letters, Jell-O salad
recipes, proof that she had paid the Texas poll tax in 1960,
brightly spangled invitations to cocktail parties from hosts
long dead. The attic was an overflowing archive, and a majority of the documents originated with me. Here they all

were—the stories I had been drawing and writing from the time I could hold a crayon in my fist. They had titles such as "Misery of Death" (Parts One through Four) and "The Life and Death of Sandy the Cocker Spaniel," the last based on fact, being the sad tale of a babysitter's puppy, a station wagon, and Washtenaw Avenue. In a similar vein, I created "The Man Ran Over," which opened with a moviegoer watching a film about someone being killed by a car. Leaving the theater, he sees a fatal accident and reflects grimly on what he had been watching onscreen a few moments before—life replicating art in little stick figures.

Every now and then, my father would take dictation and type out one of my doom-laden narratives:

> Fane was a man who was killed when he was a
>   boy.
> He decided that he could make them think he
>   was alive by making a model of himself.
> They knew that he was a brave boy and could do
>   a lot of things.
> And after that they knew that he was brave
>   enough to go and kill a bear.
> They knew that he couldn't be killed.
> Because he had armor on.
> And they thought that armor could keep them
>   from being killed.
> But they were wrong.
> And he was killed.
> THE END.

At nine, writing shakily in semi-mastered cursive script, I attempted my first autobiography, a decidedly curious few pages devoted almost exclusively to the losses I had sustained: my grandfather, Mrs. Callahan, and my maternal grandmother, Elizabeth Latimer Thaxton, who died of pancreatic cancer in the summer of 1962 after a long, closely observed yellowing. We had gone back to San Diego for her last months, and I slept with Gaga while my mother spent most of her time over at the hospital. Early each morning, as the planes started up their infernal diving, the phone would ring and a conversation ensue, after which I would ask if my other grandmother was still living. The question grew to be reflexive and almost meaningless, just part of the daily routine, until the Sunday that Gaga shocked me by shaking her head, putting down the phone, and breaking into tears.

(Eventually, all four of my grandparents would occupy ground in the same cemetery, which I imagine is an unusual statistic for somebody of my generation and atomized world. Gaga lived the longest, and probably could have lived longer had she not decided to stop eating and drinking during a hospitalization in the summer of 1983. But she was tired, she knew what she was doing, and I respected her for it. I spoke to her a few days before her death, and she was philosophical: "Give me new eyes, new ears, new knees, and a new bladder and I'll go on for another eighty-nine years.")

Of all the writings and drawings I found in the family attic, the most representative may be a psychological self-portrait drawn when I was eleven—a macabre, wretchedly rendered stick figure wearing a crown, smiling, with a cartoon speech bubble that reads, "Everyone loves me!" Unfortunately, all unbeknownst to the smug naïf, a bomb is plummeting directly above his head, he is sipping from a cup marked "Poison," a knife and a bullet are hurtling toward him, a grenade and the black ball of fused dynamite associated with anarchists in old movies are just to his side, waiting to detonate, while a rattlesnake (helpfully labeled "Rattlesnake") crawls around his feet, preparing to strike.

By then, my father's zigzag pursuit of tenure had pulled him from Michigan to a deanship in Denton, Texas, and, when I was seven, to a full professorship at the University of Connecticut in Storrs, forever my hometown and the setting for most of the rest of this story.

Northeastern Connecticut residents take a slightly defensive pride in the area. This is not the suburban Connecticut of the coastal cities and towns, built with New York wealth and packed with commuters and yachts. Nor is it the storybook Connecticut of the Berkshires, with its majestic homes, historical plaques, and manicured village greens. Northeastern Connecticut, one of the less affluent corners of New England, has its own sober beauty, made up of brambles, stones, low hills, and bleary skies—a beauty most apparent on monochromatic afternoons in deep winter, when the snow has hardened on the ground, dusk sets in by four, and a crack of winter light shines through the woods, accompanied by the rattle of distant buzz saws.

Storrs compressed the world into two or three miles; there was a single grocery store, a movie theater that re-

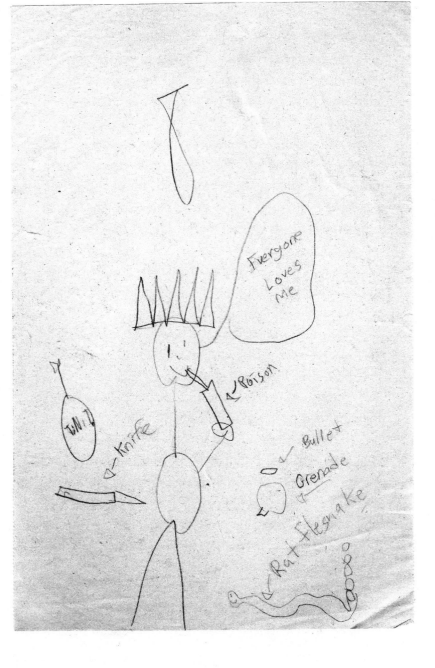

ceived box-office hits a year late, a record and radio shop (my favorite), an unusually fine concert series, the comparatively big city of Hartford to visit once or twice a year, and a handful of people whom I determined I would know forever. My mother, accustomed to California sunshine and sophisticated window shopping, took a long time to get used to Storrs; my father was oblivious to location as long as he could pursue his work; for my brother and sister, it was simply a good place to grow up. I still visit whenever possible, for there is no other place I can ever know in such intimate detail—its genealogy, its pathways, its history, and its legends.

Legends: What better start than the structure on the northwest corner of Route 195 and Birchwood Heights, a peculiar monument to fraternal hatred? Sprawling and uncared for, the proverbial "haunted house," it had been left to brothers who despised each other. But they continued to live there, dividing their legacy precisely in half, painting exterior sections in clashing shades of blue, even arranging the shingles so as to run in different directions, all the time refusing any manner of social contact. Eventually they both died, and the house stood vacant for many years before it was torn down in the late 1960s. The last time I passed by, nothing had been built in its stead.

Then there was the man who had been driving with his much-loved wife and somehow there had been an accident and she was killed. From that day on, or so we were told, he swore that he would never again ride in a car, and we would regularly see him walking from his home in Mansfield Center three or four miles to work in Willimantic, his face a fixed mask of astonished, unreachable pain. Everybody in town knew the lore; still, in snow or stormy weather, locals would pull over and offer him a ride. And he perpetually refused, sometimes quite brusquely, and continued his solitary penance, growing ever more stooped with the years until he vanished altogether.

The nearest town of any size, Willimantic, was a tough place then, and there was nobody tougher than Frank G., who led a local motorcycle gang. Frank met a remarkable end. Along with one of his droogs, he had kidnapped a young woman, forced her a few hundred feet from the main road, and raped her repeatedly. Her cries attracted the attention of a rescue team, and Frank was soon fleeing through the woods, of which there were then a great deal. Meanwhile, a resident of neighboring Chaplin seemed to be having a rough day. He had been phoning the police all morning, insisting that men from Mars were preparing to land on his roof and that he intended to shoot as many as he could before they dragged him away. Right then, Frank G., panting hard and believing he had escaped, darted out of the forest and into the wrong backyard, where he came face to face with Karma.

This is only a sampling of the tales still relayed late at night in local bars, usually followed by a shake of the head and some morsel of homegrown philosophy, such as "Only in *Storrs*, man!"

For a time in my twenties, after my parents moved away and I had settled in New York, I subscribed to the *Willimantic Chronicle* ("Your Hometown Newspaper Since 1877"), which I'd read since childhood. There was a lag of three or four days before the paper arrived in the mailbox, and Manhattan delivery was priced at a then exorbitant seventy-seven dollars for a year's subscription, but the investment was well worth it. I did not choose the *Chronicle* for its coverage of world affairs, which editors invariably cribbed from the wire services. It was the local news, the stories no other paper printed, that I cared about, for the *Chronicle* kept me in touch, however vicariously, with the people and the landscape I had then known for more than a quarter of a century.

I would speed under midtown on the IRT subway, my thoughts 120 miles away, as I read about Storrs in the *Chronicle.* I might be touched by a photograph of a Brownie troop, by the identical eyes in one young girl that I had once loved in her mother. I would be saddened by the obituary of a beloved teacher, not surprised by the arrest of a former nemesis, upset that the antique neon sign at the grocery, one or two years away from the stature of a classic, had been unceremoniously demolished, amused that the trailer park where I once lived in impoverished splendor had been razed and replaced by spiffy condominiums.

When last I returned, I picked up a copy of the *Chronicle,* and it was as though the clocks had stopped. The front page featured a picture of a tin bucket and suckling spigot on a weathered tree, harvesting the seasonal supply of maple syrup. In the background was a long stone wall, laced with the rusty barbed wire that has run through Storrs since the nineteenth century. I reflected that I once knew that wall by heart, knew exactly which rocks would support the full weight of a sprinting child, as I dashed down to the brook with my brother, Rick. And I realized that mine was in many ways a classic New England boyhood, of the sort believed extinct even then, complete with swimming holes and Saturday-morning tobogganing on a slope called Horsebarn Hill.

Occasionally I wander through the cemetery high above North Eagleville Road and recognize all the original town names—Thompson, Oldershaw, Stearns, and, of course, Storrs (the college had been constructed on family land). Every time I visit the graveyard, I come across somebody else whom I once knew, most recently the friendly lady with the shadow of a mustache who collected our lunch tickets at Storrs Grammar School. And I am old enough to put actual faces to the names on the campus buildings—Jorgensen, Gentry, Gant, Babbidge—as they went up during a time when universities honored people who had given their lives, rather than a mere hunk of freshly minted cash, to the institution.

It was in Storrs that both my talents and my problems initially attracted attention. My father had been professionally fascinated with standardized testing for several years by that point, and I had become his laboratory of choice. I can hear his voice through this entry in my mother's diary, written when I was three: "A brilliant day for our boy! Ellis had some time after classes yesterday which he devoted to Tim. Part of the time was spent testing him for verbal comprehension. He had been tested before—six or so months before but not since. This time he answered all the questions perfectly!! For comparison's sake—only 2% of 5-year-olds got 19 out of 20!! Ellis also tested him by asking him to draw a man. Only non-recognizable scrawls were evident until Ellis drew a rectangle lengthwise on the paper. Timmy for the first time actually drew!—arms, legs, a head, a hat, navel and even 'bowels' in appropriate number and location."

By the time I was eight or nine, I had discovered that if I could make my father laugh he could not be angry with me. And so I grew adept at charming adults, with a sort of anxious, breathless, balls-in-the-air kind of wit. My father began taking me to his classes, once a year, to perform as a burgeoning genius. Mansfield Training School, the state's leading educational facility for people then classified as "mentally retarded," was down the road, and some of its residents would be brought in toward the end of the semester in order to demonstrate the difficulties involved in their instruction. The next week was my turn, and I'd breeze into the classroom, prove my intellectual prowess by reading random passages of the students' textbooks aloud, and offer blithe nuggets of sage kiddy wisdom, in the manner of the early *Peanuts*, with which I was then very much taken.

I'd like to pretend that I didn't enjoy these appearances but, truth be told, they served to confirm my "specialness," which was very important to me. After all, geniuses were granted enormous latitude; they could even cut off their ears if they wanted to, although that particular action had limited appeal. Still, there was a catch, as my father would reiterate shortly before each class: *never*, under any circumstances, could I let on that I was related to him, let alone that I was his son, which he thought would be an unforgivable bit of braggadocio. And so the plan had me refer to him exclusively as "Dr. Page," as though he had found me through some Agency for gifted children or something.

This ruse worked for a while, though I was always an inept actor. But there came a day when I was chattering happily about the old opera stars whose records I had recently grown to love—Enrico Caruso, Geraldine Farrar, Rosa Ponselle, Feodor Chaliapin . . .

"And who was Chaliapin, Timmy?" my father coaxed.

"Oh, he was a great Russian bass," I replied, pronouncing the last word as though Chaliapin were a fish rather than the possessor of an especially low male singing voice.

The class broke into laughter. I reddened and grew agitated, having no idea what I had done, yet knowing that my dignity had been sorely affronted.

"That's pronounced *'base,'* " my father said, chuckling, too.

"I've never heard anybody say the word before," I answered, truthfully and with no little desperation. "I read about him in my opera book and on the back of my record, Dad!"

Dad—the magic syllable, and I knew I'd made a terrible mistake the instant the word slid out. The classroom laughter redoubled, and I cannot recall how my father explained himself. We rode home in silence and I don't think I was punished, but I was never again invited to another one of his classes.

I fared no better in my own schooling. If I wasn't deeply interested in a subject, I couldn't concentrate on it at all— that dreadful algebra, those Bunsen burners, the mystifying and deservedly extinct slide rule! Late in each quarter, when it became obvious to me that I had no clue to what I was supposed to have learned, I'd attend some makeup sessions and try desperately to pay attention. As the teacher rattled on, I would grind my teeth, twirl the tops of my socks around my index finger—once, I poked myself repeatedly through my pocket with a pin—anything to keep my mind engaged. But it was impossible: a leaf would float past the open window, or I'd notice the pattern of veins on a girl's hand, or a shout from the playground would trigger a set of irresistible associations that carried me back to another day.

And then the dream was ruptured by the sound of a bell; the class was irrevocably over, and I knew no more about the associative property of multiplication or beryllium than I did an hour before. Failure was assured and the countdown began to the Dies Irae, when my report card would arrive and land me in trouble again, for my father was incredulous that a boy who blithely recited the names and dates of all the United States' presidents and their wives in order (backward upon request) couldn't manage to pass elementary math and science.

My grades only worsened as teachers expected more of me. I still have a school report on "Making a Living in the Amazon," on which we had been required to work for a week. My contribution read, in its entirety: "In the dense, rainy, rain forest, it is hard to make a living. One way is fishing in the river that is from a mile wide to a 100 miles wide. Brazil nut collecting is another way. You can gather manioc. You are very limited as to what to do for a living in the Amazon rain forest."

Limited, indeed—I doubt that I had even bothered to find out what manioc was—and, of course, I flunked. But I *was* learning some things. I probably knew more about true crime than any other fifth grader in Storrs, and I could discourse for several minutes about the Al Capone–decreed 1929 St. Valentine's Day Massacre at 2122 North Clark Street in Chicago. I took to the piano naturally and joyfully, and was composing before I formally knew how. I was able to storm through idiosyncratic renditions of most of Chopin's easier piano pieces and the simpler passages in his larger works, and I could correctly identify all his opus numbers. I finished my first novel—fifty pages of it, filled with a narrative invention that I've never been able to recapture. (The manuscript was lost long ago, but I do recall, with some amusement, that I killed off my central character, a cat, by having him eat "badly prepared fish.")

Still, what was any teacher to make of a report like this one, after we were asked, in class, to write about something that we had at home? Most of my classmates wrote about dolls or toys or maybe a BB gun. I produced the following, from memory:

> At our house we have many records. One of the
> most interesting is a collection of old opera
> records called "Golden Age Ensembles" (RCA
> Victor LCT 1003). The oldest was made in
> 1909, the latest in 1932. I will give you the
> bands on the record: Band one gives an example
> of German opera with Schumann, Schorr,
> Melchior, Parr and Williams—date 1932. Band

two is the "Miserere" from "Il Trovatore" with Caruso and Alda—date 1910. Band 3 is from "Samson et Dalila"—Caruso, Journet, and Homer made this in 1919. Band four is from "La Boheme" with Scotti and Farrar. Date 1909. Band 5 is the "Sextet" from "Lucia" with Caruso, Bada, Journet, de Luca, Galli-Curci and Egener. Date 1917. Band six is the Quartet from "Rigoletto" with Caruso, Galli-Curci, De Luca and Perini. Date 1917 on the same day as the "Sextet" recorded in Camden, New Jersey. Band seven is the "Masked Ball" quintet with Caruso, Rothier, Hempel, Duchene and de Segurola— date 1914. Band 8 is "La Virgine degli Angeli" with Pinza and Ponselle. Date 1928. So now you have heard about it. I hope you will hear it and buy it.

By then, I was choosy about the records I played and both terrified and tantalized by the way they restored Enrico Caruso and Nellie Melba to life for a few minutes, ghostly visitors who had returned, accompanied by tinny orchestras (outfitted, for acoustical purposes, with tubas instead of lower strings) to sing for me through a hiss of shellac and antiquity. The operatic picture sleeves bewitched me— photographs of handsome mustachioed men in awkward costumes, crazed sopranos in impractical gowns. A kindly librarian at the University of Connecticut, recognizing starvation when she saw it, extended lending privileges, and I read all the opera books in the collection: Dorothy Caruso's two biographies of her husband, Melba's *Melodies and Memories,* Frances Alda's *Men, Women and Tenors* (probably the liveliest of the bunch), and Geraldine Farrar's *Such Sweet Compulsion,* which had the bizarre distinction of supposedly being half written by the singer and half dictated from the grave by her dead mother.

The younger Farrar was then still living, and I wrote her a childish love letter. "Dear Miss Farrar," it began, "although I am only ten years old, I think your singing is wonderful." To make sure I impressed her with my maturity, I typed the note, though this added many hours to its composition time. Barely daring to expect an answer, I mailed the finished missive to her, care of RCA Victor, for whom she had recorded half a century earlier. And she wrote back, her letter reaching me on a snowy January morning—an affectionate reply in her eccentric and inimitable scrawl, signed "With every blessing." The letter went immediately into a frame, but I took it out fifteen or twenty times a day for some weeks afterward in order to hold the precious document in my hands.

I tried to get Rick excited about these new interests, and regularly brought him up to the music library on Saturday mornings, as soon as our never-to-be-missed weekly fest of Popeye and the Three Stooges on Channel 10 had concluded. Once there, we would sign out a lot of records and I'd put them on a turntable in the listening room and instruct him: "Listen—this is Elisabeth Schumann singing Bach; listen to the purity of her sound! This is Wanda

Landowska playing Handel, and that instrument is the harpsichord!" Rick was good-humored about it all, but he was six years old and didn't really understand. Later, as an adult, he told me that he used to wonder idly how much time would pass before he'd grow up and want to do this with *his* weekends.

THREE

A "Loving Family Group"—flanked by my father, Rick,
Betsy, and my mother, early 1960s, place unknown.

"There's a world outside of Yonkers!"

My patrician mother loved this line from *Hello, Dolly!*,
and, in turn, she insisted that her children learn about the
world outside Storrs. She treated Betsy to a weekend stay at
the Ritz-Carlton in Boston, where they enjoyed a full-
course luncheon amid refined surroundings. I had my
chance as well. After the announcement that New York's
original Metropolitan Opera House would close in the
spring of 1966, with demolition slated for the following
year, my mother escorted me down on the train to attend
the soprano Licia Albanese's penultimate Met performance

of *Madama Butterfly* and visit the place where so much musical history had been made.

There we met up with my great-aunt Jeanne, a fiercely independent woman who had lived in New York by herself for half a century and who had not only heard Caruso sing but had heard him in Ludovic Halévy's *La Juive* at the Met on the night of December 24, 1920—his final appearance anywhere, as she and I both knew. I considered her one of the anointed and demanded that she relay as many memories of the night as she could summon. And then we all traveled to the Willoughby-Peerless camera shop near Penn Station to hunt for silent films that could be purchased for about six dollars and taken home to show on the family 8mm home-movie projector.

I had discovered silent films during an earlier trip to Hartford. A few times a year, my mother would dress us up—Betsy in Sunday finery, Rick and me in clip-on ties and sport jackets made of one hundred percent rayon, a little grease in our hair—and we would spend a day in what seemed to us, before New York, a very big city indeed. Hartford had already been mortally wounded by the Interstate Highway System—which had blown up downtown, bulldozed much of the historic district, effectively walled off the traditional African-American neighborhood, and closed pedestrian access to the Connecticut River, which had been the city's lifeline from its founding. Nevertheless, even in decline Hartford still had a few attractions: a Peanut Shoppe bursting with sweet confections; an ancient restaurant called Honiss's Oyster House, which conspicuously maintained a men's bar, complete with spittoons, through the 1960s; and a grand old department store called G. Fox & Company, established in 1847 and widely presumed to be immortal practically until the day it closed.

In its prime, G. Fox offered everything from a rare-coin-and-stamp shop to a photographer's studio and a formal restaurant, peopled almost entirely by well-dressed middle-aged women wearing hats and heavy perfume. I habitually veered directly toward the ninth floor, where the record department was, or to the bookstore on the mezzanine, while the rest of the family shopped for clothes or something even more boring. It was in the mezzanine that I started reading a remaindered volume called *Classics of the Silent Screen,* credited to the longtime radio and TV host Joe Franklin but actually written in close collaboration with William K. Everson, America's pioneering historian of early film. My mother paid $2.98 for the book; I knew it by heart within a week.

Silent films became the visual complement to my old records. Hours flew by at the UConn library as I researched the lives of actors and actresses on microfilm, inscribing their birth and death years in my copy of *Classics of the Silent Screen,* and I recall the genuine sense of mourning I felt when I came across Barbara La Marr's sad, youthful face on an obituary page from 1926. Not surprisingly, *Sunset Boulevard,* that witty, resplendently creepy evocation of primordial Hollywood, counted as my favorite "talkie" (I actually called them that—in 1965!), and I regularly set the clock and woke in the middle of the night to watch Chester

Conklin or Louise Dresser take on minor roles in some B movie that the low-signal Worcester, Massachusetts, station put on when nobody else was watching.

There was definitely a morbid streak in all this. One of the reasons I was so interested in the late nineteenth and early twentieth centuries was that singers and actors were suddenly able, in a tangible way, to immortalize themselves. They were *still there,* somehow—technically dead, of course, but also preserved forever, as I wanted so much to be. I believed in photographs and movies in a way that I never believed in drawings or paintings. For me, photographs represented a factual connection to what I deemed to be real life, while visual art was just personal fantasy, no matter how brilliantly accomplished. A single crude black-and-white photograph of Frédéric Chopin exists, yet I felt a ghostly communion with the picture of the dying composer and prized it far above the florid, romantic, and elaborately colored image by his friend Eugène Delacroix.

I was temperamentally attracted to black and white, which seemed to me more expressive than color. This was the epoch of filmic spectacle, and David Lean's *Lawrence of Arabia* had recently been released, to great acclaim from all the critics, including the one who mattered most to me: my father. Eventually, *Lawrence of Arabia* arrived at the College Theater and I simply hated it—for its noise, its bigness, the brightness of its colors, the everlasting swelling of the orchestra, all of which I found alarming and unpleasant affronts. I was much more at home alone in my darkened basement with the steady, reassuring *clickety-clack* of the projector, and I'd sit through my growing collection of silent films—Charlie Chaplin, Buster Keaton, Lupino Lane, Andy Clyde—again and again.

I'd watch the family movies, too—no longer frightened by visions of my grandfather and my grandmother but wishing instead to somehow communicate with them through the flickering dust of their images on a screen. Mine was the last generation to inhabit a time when old films, old photographs, and old recordings inescapably looked and sounded just as old as they were. Setting aside any fashion considerations, pictures of my grandparents or even my parents in their youth seemed to originate in another world—the big, cardboard-like prints, the formal poses, the mezzotints. Snapshots from the 1950s and the 1960s looked somewhat better but were mostly over- or underexposed, and home movies were brief, silent, fuzzy, and fragmented.

But I grew up as media grew up, and by the time video recording was easily accessible to consumers, in the 1980s, life could be preserved pretty much as it happened. My children can watch hours upon hours of themselves and others on long-ago vacations, at birthday parties, preparing for graduation, or living through ordinary evenings at home, temporary hit songs playing in the background, with sounds and visuals so clear that they might have been recorded yesterday. This immediacy, now attained, will never disappear, even when all the players are dead. That, too, will be pretty spooky.

Silent film has remained a primary interest of mine. A few years ago, Kino Video issued everything that was released by the pioneering Thomas Edison Company from

1891 to 1918, hundreds of early snippets, rowdy and teeming with life. They include images of gymnasts and athletes, cockfights and boxing matches, firemen racing furiously toward hotel fires, the night lights of Coney Island, and any number of streetscapes from a vanished Manhattan. A man sneezes—the most banal action in the world—but it is now captured forever. Annie Oakley shoots at glass balls tossed into the air, while the trapeze artist Charmion, suspended high above the ground, removes her clothes in front of some eager spectators. An exotic dancer named Fatima, who had been a sensation at the 1896 World's Fair, wriggles seductively in a dance considered so risqué that it was censored (somebody superimposed what looks like a white picket fence over her splendid gyrations); and, in an early special-effects illusion, Mary, Queen of Scots, appears to lose her head. There is newsreel footage from the Spanish-American War and from the Galveston Flood. Primitive oil drills bow up and down like mournful, nodding mantises. And, in one decidedly odd scene that is difficult to watch even a hundred years later, an aged elephant is taken into a pit and summarily electrocuted, roaring silently and collapsing onto its side amid a puff of smoke.

Most of these are interesting, but none of them is art: the movies were still a fancy toy. And then, suddenly, in late 1903, came *The Great Train Robbery*, the American cinema's first defining masterpiece. Directed by Edwin S. Porter, this twelve-minute epic is an archetype for both the crime film and the Western (despite its central–New Jersey locations). The story, told without titles, couldn't be much simpler— bad guys hold up a train, escape and frolic with their ill-gotten gains for a while, and are finally caught and killed—but stationary vignette gave way to active storytelling, and a new bond was forged between filmmaker and viewer.

I became obsessed with *The Great Train Robbery* and was thrilled when my mother uncovered an 8mm print during one of her New York jaunts. One thing exasperated me, though. Either in a dubious attempt to re-copyright its own version of an out-of-copyright film or simply to make for a more contemporary viewing experience, the company that had reissued *The Great Train Robbery* for home projection had diced it up, crosscutting between scenes in a style that I knew did not become common until at least 1908, with the advent of D. W. Griffith's early shorts for the Biograph Company.

This was sacrilege. So I went to the library and unearthed a complete scene-by-scene description of *The Great Train Robbery* as it had been released in 1903. Then I returned to my basement, took out my viewer and splicing tape, and recut the doctored version back into Edwin S. Porter's original conception, with its long unbroken scenes left intact. I remain proud of my youthful outrage, and of the steps I took to assuage it. Had a teacher known about or understood what I was doing, this might have demonstrated a seriousness of purpose that I could never quite grant to manioc.

My fascination with the technical side of old movies also stemmed from the stark and still disturbing Abraham Zapruder film of the assassination of John F. Kennedy. No one was actually permitted to view the 26.6-second snippet back then, but *Life* magazine, which owned the rights, published enlarged still photographs from it shortly after Kennedy's death, then brought them out again for the release of the Warren Report and thereafter whenever any kind of conspiracy controversy bubbled to the surface. The frames were numbered, and the fatal shot hit Kennedy's head at No. 313—a bright, ghastly spray of red and white. I dreamed, not once but several times, that I somehow stopped the world for a moment at frame No. 312—a precious fragment of a second before the horror—and, in so doing, was able to correct history. (JFK, when next I saw him, was extravagantly grateful, and I got to play with Caroline and her pony.)

Most of my other dreams were less eventful. There was a wood next to our house, and I used to imagine that I could turn off the Gurleyville path and arrive in some hitherto unsuspected fifteenth-century English or Bavarian village, with thatched roofs and a lot of cheerful, industrious people who liked me and had me feast with them at a long table, as they burst regularly into song. It was all a little like *Brigadoon,* which I don't believe I'd yet seen. I also dreamed that I could fly, soaring through the air with the same technique used to swim underwater, an exuberant breaststroke that defied gravity.

But the most vivid dream featured Mabel Normand, the athletic daredevil of the silent film, whose life would be destroyed by her association with the director William Desmond Taylor. Taylor was shot to death at 404 South Alvarado Street in Los Angeles on February 1, 1922, by an unknown assailant, and in the past two decades, at least three books on this murder have been published, all proposing different culprits, so the case clearly remains of more than academic interest. My dream Mabel was young and strong and carried me on her back around Hollywood; she even introduced me to Ford Sterling, the "koppo di tutti koppi" of the Keystone Kops. I loved Mabel, felt safe with her, and wanted to live with her forever. When I woke up and remembered that this miraculous new friend—so real that I felt I could not only touch but ride her until a moment before—had actually died in 1930, I was disconsolate for the rest of the day.

Jean Harlow appeared in only a couple of silent films before the advent of sound, but I didn't hold that against her. 1965 saw the release of two terrible biographical movies about Harlow, one with Carroll Baker, the other with Carol Lynley. In an attempt to cash in on the Harlow revival, Dell Publishing reissued a magazine-size biography of the actress that had been written several decades earlier by Louella O. Parsons, the syndicated movie columnist for the Hearst newspapers. I now bought and absorbed the booklet. (Browsing at the record store shortly thereafter, I was delighted to spy it amid the coffee-table clutter on the cover of Bob Dylan's *Bringing It All Back Home* album—which is the unusual and just possibly unique route by which I grew interested in Dylan.)

I began writing my own stapled books on manila paper about invented movie stars in my own universe. The first one was devoted to "Jean Herold," and I produced what I titled a memorial volume, with lots of crudely drawn pictures in place of the publicity shots that filled the Parsons book. I determined that Herold, too, should be a star who died young, remembered with fondness by her friends Flute Henzi and Sheralyn du Bois, as well as by her last boyfriend, Shonglato McShea, who, in my Parsons-like prose, never recovered from her loss, despite the fact that he outlived her by thirty-one years—William Powell to Herold's Harlow.

Yet current popular culture repulsed me; I would read and emulate Parsons on Harlow but never Hedda Hopper on Elizabeth Taylor, a minor blessing, I suppose. "I despise the Beatles and their ilk," my Blimpish younger self proclaimed in a school paper shortly after the group's first appearance on *The Ed Sullivan Show*, when other boys my age were growing their hair long and learning to play the guitar. My favorite pop musician then was the Scottish comedian Harry Lauder, a star in vaudeville and music halls at the beginning of the past century, who told obscure jokes in brogue and sang through exaggerated hiccups in a state of feigned intoxication. The depth of my admiration for Lauder now baffles me as much as the steady diet of horehound drops I adopted as snack food, or my insistence, much of one autumn, that I thread a rabbit's foot through each buttonhole of my shirt, which I kept tightly fastened to the neck. But nobody could have persuaded me to abandon these quirks, and any attempt to do so would have been taken as a physical threat and reduced me to hysteria.

Eventually, I realized that I could go to the nurse's office if I became overstimulated. It was quiet there, and I could lie down in a darkened room and be alone, and soon I would make any excuse I could to find that peace. Some of my teachers thought this was a ploy for attention. I have since concluded that it was, in fact, a survival tactic, for it allowed me to try to settle my own hubbub, away from the jangling, jarring hubbub of others. One nurse in particular took an interest in me, asked me questions, and served as my de facto psychiatrist, but I ended up making her cross. She kept saying "confidentially," and I didn't know what the word meant, having heard it only in an old Merrie Melodies cartoon, uttered by some brassy agent type with a big cigar. So I didn't realize that she was asking me to keep our sessions strictly between the two of us, and I went and bragged about them to my parents and the other students, after which I was left alone once more, for my father thought psychiatry was hooey and made formal objection to such treatment.

A friend published a sweet autobiography titled *Thank You, Everyone,* in which she expressed gratitude to everybody who had influenced her, ranging from Woody Allen to my sister Betsy. If I were to create a similar book, I would call it *Sorry, Everyone,* and apologize for my youthful cluelessness. To the shy girl with the protruding jawbone (it never occurred to me that she would not share my enthusiasm for her unusually simian features). To the boy who came over to my house in the middle of my Caruso phase and endured a precious weekend afternoon comparing recordings of *Celeste Aida.* And, later on, to the perplexed young women who might have become lovers had I understood that their sudden friendship had any sort of physical impetus. Instead, I chattered on about this and that, looking away, and soon they vanished, in search of more game and grounded potential partners. Sorry, everyone. I didn't understand.

It was hard for me to be touched. I froze when I was hugged by anybody who was not a relative, and I made love like the Tin Man until I was well into adulthood. Like many children, I recoiled when fundamental facts about the reproduction of the species were explained to me. (Typically for the time and the place, there was no suggestion that new pleasures might be involved, and the physical act, examined through an anxious, presexual eye, sounded bizarre.) Shortly after this enlightenment, my parents threw a party, attended by their closest friends, whose athletic, fortyish bodies, properly clothed, I watched in mortified amazement. I took a silent recount of their children. Oh, my God, I thought. They did *that* three times!

Some of this queasiness surely stemmed from the fact that I was a product of the inhibited 1950s, an era of demonstrable public insanity. When we weren't plowing superhighways through the centers of long-settled cities or preparing citizens to "survive" a direct nuclear attack, we were being told by advertising firms and the corporations they served that breast-feeding was both outdated and barbaric, something to be ashamed of. My mother, bless her, bucked the trend, but a lot of lonely babies were denied the primal human contact that should be our first gift from the outer world and, instead, condemned to drink stirred-up white sludge from cold rubber nipples, which was said to be both more modern and more "hygienic." How bizarre that it was just at the moment when the primary biological function of women's breasts was least valued that amply bosomed stars like Marilyn Monroe, Jane Russell, and Jayne Mansfield came to be seen as the apogee of sex appeal!

Anything related to the human body, especially mine, seemed to me bad news, with physical education at the top of the page. Once or twice a week, I would be herded out to play kickball; teams were chosen, and I was embedded among the strongest kids, to provide some chance of even battle. In memory, the game is forever bases loaded with two outs when my turn at the plate comes, and I am as well suited as a giraffe to meet the big red ball that rolls toward me with frightening speed.

Still, for a moment the same people who generally disdained or bullied me became my friends, cheering me on to hitherto unsuspected athletic glory: "You can do it, Tim!" If I could make the ball lose its gravity, as my best pal, Annie, did so effortlessly with those balletic *whomps* from her long, gracefully muscled legs, I might redeem myself. Our gym teacher, Miss B.—scowling, beefy, and, after four decades, the only person in the world I just might swerve to hit on a deserted road—had no such illusions and waited for the inevitable, with her festering contempt and ready whistle. Grinning stupidly, shirttail out and flapping, underwear pulled halfway up my back, I would lope toward the ball, which would eventually collide with my ankle or heel and then bounce off into the woods or into the waiting arms of the catcher. My chance was up, and I was a freak once more.

"*So?*" I wanted to scream. "There are things that I *know*; things that I can *do.* Can you name the duet from *La Bohème* that Antonio Scotti and Geraldine Farrar recorded in Camden, New Jersey, on October 6, 1909? What was the New York address of D. W. Griffith's first studio? How many books by *David Graham Phillips* have you read? Who was

Adelaide *Crapsey*? I learned to play Chopin's entire Prelude in E Minor in a single night!" And then tears, of course, so the taunts redoubled.

The school was perplexed by my behavior, for it was increasingly obvious that I was not "normal," especially by the straitened standards of the mid-1960s. I have sometimes wondered whether the stratospheric IQ scores with which I was credited were nudged upward by my father, the tester who administered my most triumphant examinations. Whatever the case, while Rick and Betsy soared through school, academically and socially, I lagged consistently at or near the bottom of the class, decidedly out of control—half asleep or aggressively assertive—much of the time.

In the sixth grade, however, I found a way to both indulge my interest in silent movies and exert direct social control over my classmates. I saved up the five dollars necessary to buy fifty feet of 8mm film, then borrowed my father's ancient Revere home-movie camera, a legacy from his own father, and shot a slapstick comedy called *A Little Fight*. I dedicated the four-minute film to the memory of Mack Sennett and, paying proper homage, received a pie in my face twice. The "pies" were tins filled with Reddi Whip, and the sweet froth spread ear to ear in a delicious and unsettling sensory explosion that I can still taste.

We took the finished movie up to Storrs Drug to send off to a lab, and then waited an interminable week for its development. Alas, something had malfunctioned when I loaded the canister, or I had erred in my arrangement of the camera lenses, or maybe we'd just purchased a bum roll. In any event, my first film came back absolutely blank, without a single image on it. "You would have thought we'd been filming Negroes at midnight," I wrote cheekily in one of my many books about our production company, not then knowing any "Negroes"—a safely polite, if already staid, word for African-Americans in 1966.

We tried again a few weeks later. This time, everything worked out and we had ourselves a movie. From then on, every third or fourth Saturday was consecrated to filmmaking, and I would invite both friends from the neighborhood and people with whom I wanted to become friends, with potential stardom as my come-on. It is a rare preteen who doesn't fantasize, at least on occasion, about becoming a movie personality, and that's what I was offering in my own, localized way. I controlled the camera, I composed the script, I chose the actors, I barked the orders, I edited the film, and I invited everybody back to the house a couple of weeks later, for screening and a cast party. Anybody who wanted to be involved could take it or leave it.

Several of our titles were borrowed or adapted directly from historical predecessors: *The Immigrant, The Fall of a Nation,* and *The Widow's Villa.* D. W. Griffith had got his start at the Biograph Company; another early company was called Vitagraph, and so I compromised and named our troupe Viograph. (Bite-a-Graph would have sounded terrible.) I strove for longer and longer statements—splicing together three or four fifty-foot rolls of film for a running time of twelve to fifteen minutes. One film, on which we worked for the better part of a week during a school vacation, was a full half hour long, saddled with the stunningly anti-euphonious title *Behn Pohs, Filmmaker.*

My father offered some important criticism around this time, and it has influenced everything I've done since. I was in the habit of narrating my films while they were projected, and one night he told me to stop and let him watch without any commentary. "You're not always going to be here to explain your work," he said. "It has to stand by itself." After the premiere of *Behn Pohs, Filmmaker,* my magnum opus, my father told me that he hadn't understood the story at all and that nobody else would, either. I was hurt by his words and built myself up into an uncontrollable crying jag. But the next day I calmly added some new subtitles to make the film more coherent, vastly improving it in the process. (To this day, while I admire poetic opacity in certain authors and filmmakers, I cannot tolerate it in my own work. You may or may not like something I've written, but I'll do my damnedest to ensure that you know what I wanted to say.)

Several figures stood out in the Viograph cast: Michael Flynn, a piano-playing friend, darkly handsome and the best actor of the lot; my brother, Rick, sensitive and understated; the family across the street (Debra, Tommy, Matthew, and Rebecca Brooks); pretty Amy Sandberg; and Dean Cook, a great friend and an enthusiastic collaborator, who was later killed, as were so many of my classmates, by the impaired judgment of a drunk driver. And, finally, there was Annie, my kickball heroine, about whom more later.

I wrote detailed, surprisingly objective critiques of our films, some of them quite brutal. Here are my thoughts on *The Affairs of Peter Lawcerse,* which, I noted, had been "released" on November 13, 1966: "This is the stupid and unintelligible story of a man who has an affair with his mother and is finally shot by his best friend's wife. Bad sets, bad acting, bad photography. . . ." But I liked most of *The Immigrant:* "From the beginning, everything works. All acting, except for Tim Page, is perfect. The film merits comparison with every film up to *Opus 21* [which I made a year later] and nearly all after. It is short and to the point and can still move a sensitive viewer."

And I mimicked a feature that has been running in Sunday newspapers for some fifty years now—the celebrity question-and-answer column called "Walter Scott's Personality Parade." There I addressed such deathless questions as "Is Betsy Page off the screen for good, now that her contract has expired?" ("She hasn't renewed it," I replied to myself tersely—we must have had a tiff.) I wrote capsule, breathlessly hyped biographies of all my players: "Dean Cook is probably the fastest growing star in the industry. His first picture was the recent *The Fall of a Nation,* in which he gave such a fine performance that his position with the finer actors was assured." Or—my favorite—"Becca Brooks is Debby Brooks's sister. She made her debut in the Anne Beddow film *The Widow's Villa.* She was the perfect choice for the little girl, for she has that rare thing in kindergarteners—*realism.*"

FOUR

Annie in the movies. Storrs, 1969.

DAVID HOFFMAN: "While you're directing, you really yell a lot. Now, why do you think they take all that; why do you suppose they help you out?"

TIM PAGE (after a long, smug smile): "They're hams! That's one of the reasons, at least. When I go to school, I speak about my films often—not only the films I make but the films I collect—and these people come up to me, even my worst enemies, and say, 'Hey, Page, can I be in one of your movies?' And I say, 'Sure—uh, drop by and have a screen test sometime.' We don't have screen tests, but it gets them off my back!"

From *A Day with Timmy Page* (1967),
a film by David and Iris Hoffman

In April 1967, we learned that one of Viograph's occasional actors, Paul Waxman ("a *fairly* fast growing star" was the way I qualified it), had a cousin who was a real-life professional filmmaker, based in New York. His name was David Hoffman and, with his wife, Iris, he had already produced a number of small films and was just beginning his first feature. He came up to Storrs to watch us work—we were then filming *The Fall of a Nation,* which was, as I explained to him later, the story of children who have taken over the world.

David brought along his camera equipment, loved what he saw, and returned to New York to edit his footage into a seventeen-minute documentary called *A Day with Timmy Page.* In a review for the *New York Times,* Renata Adler called *Day* a "marvelous little movie . . . made up of interviews with the young director and excerpts from his films."

> It is a microcosm of the filmmaker's world.
> "I'm known to say to the gang," Timmy
> confesses, 'Anyone got an idea for a scene?' "
> Timmy shouts a great deal, evolves several
> techniques, is a self-conscious interview and
> directs quite closely. "You," he says to a member
> of the cast, "will be sneering cruelly." He refers
> to shooting film interchangeably sometimes
> with shooting violently; he is full of ideas and
> intelligence.

A Day with Timmy Page won a number of awards, and the Eastman Kodak Company was so taken with it that I was given two cameras, a projector, and about forty rolls of the new Super 8mm film—a huge improvement over regular 8mm—to do with as I chose, as long as Kodak got a peek at the results. The all-embracing media philosophies of Marshall McLuhan were in the air, and the idea that Kodak movie cameras were now so easy that even a child could use them seemed a marvelous marketing ploy. The result was a one-minute television commercial, entitled *Kodak Visits a Young Filmmaker,* created by Hoffman and the J. Walter Thompson advertising agency and shown throughout the country in the blood-spattered springtime of 1968. Before the summer was over, I had signed my first autograph.

It was heady stuff for a brand-new teenager. *Time* magazine sent up a photographer, the celebrated David Gahr, to visit us in Storrs and I gave a long interview to a staff writer. A major story on young filmmakers had been planned and I was to have appeared prominently in it—perhaps, it had been suggested, even on the cover. Unfortunately for everybody concerned, that was the week the Democratic People's Republic of North Korea captured an American spy ship, the USS *Pueblo,* setting off an international incident and ensuring a complete overhaul of the magazine. I was heartsick when I walked into Storrs Drug after school, saw the new issue with the *Pueblo* on the cover, thumbed through it, and discovered that the young-filmmaker article had shrunk to two pages and that I had been completely eliminated (although some smart editor had the sense to include a photograph of a somewhat older but still unknown auteur by the name of George Lucas).

I hurried to the phone booth in the back of the drugstore, dialed directory assistance (always free in those days), got the number for *Time* magazine, and rang the editors in New York, demanding to know what had happened to "my" story. A very, very kind soul eventually took my call and did her best to soothe my unhappiness. I had, of course, told everybody in school—the bullies who loathed me and the teachers who flunked me—that I was going to be in *Time* that week and *they* weren't. Now I wasn't in *Time,* either, and my phone acquaintance explained that this was the way journalism worked—that nobody knew the exact contents of a newsmagazine until the very last minute. That struck me as so plausible and interesting that I immediately felt better.

My whole family was invited down to New York for the first Festival of Young Filmmakers, sponsored by Fordham University and presented in a hotel on Seventh Avenue, between Fifty-fifth and Fifty-sixth Streets, that has changed its name many times in the past forty years. It was then the Park Sheraton and, mapping it out in my head, I realized that this had to have been the site of the barbershop where the most brutal of all Murder, Inc. mafiosi, the dread Albert Anastasia, lathered up and waiting for a shave, had been assassinated eleven years earlier. A seasoned doorman, delighted to find a young man with a sense of history, confirmed my hunch and led me to what had been the barbershop, but the space was now filled with ivory statues, mostly Buddhas and elephants, at what were claimed to be the lowest prices in New York. A sign indicated that the store would be closing for good the following week, and I inquired of my new friend what the odds were that the hotel would then reconstruct the barbershop, which seemed to me a major landmark. He laughed, and told me that this particular store had been going out of business next week for at least two years.

A Day With Timmy Page inaugurated the festival. During the next few days, I would meet the producer Otto Preminger, the directors Daniel Mann and Delbert Mann (unrelated), and the actor Eli Wallach, none of whose work I knew. (They were, after all, still alive, and therefore not within my field of expertise.) McLuhan, who was recuperating from a serious illness, nevertheless traveled to New York for the occasion and, wearing a checkered bathrobe, received me in his room. He was clearly exhausted, though, and I could tell that he wanted to be left alone, so our visit was short.

On Sunday night, I appeared on live television for the first time since the third grade, when my Cub Scout troop had ventured into Hartford to go on *The Ranger Andy Show,* a local after-school cartoon program. In 1968, however, a whole network was paying attention. The Ford Foundation had recently launched something called Public Broadcast Laboratory, a live "magazine" program on Sunday nights, along the lines of what would later become *60 Minutes* but much more daring and experimental. PBL was a germinal effort to yoke together "educational stations" around the country and would eventually help lead to the formation of the Public Broadcasting System. Only a few of these programs are known to have survived (my own is still among the missing), but one dating from late April 1968 is extraordinary for the way it presents the 1960s as they pulsed and bled: interviews with African-American leaders still in shock from the three-week-old slaying of Martin Luther King, Jr.; an examination of the blooming marijuana culture that celebrates as much as it condemns; and a typically tart and incisive short film by Glenn Gould entitled *How Mozart Became a Bad Composer.*

It was exhilarating to visit New York and meet professional actors and filmmakers and talk for the better part of an hour on Channel 13 about my activities. For a little while, on that long-ago weekend, I was *home.* But then I had to go back to school—where concentration remained impossible (grade seven was the last I would manage to complete), where I was decidedly unpopular with most of my peers, where boys and girls had begun to discover each other's bodies and I could merely stand there anxious and untouched, looking at the ground and hoping somebody would approach that I could tell all about the actress Lillian Gish. ("The *World Almanac* says that she was born in 1896, but now it turns out that she might have been born in 1893—isn't that *fascinating?*")

There had been a big unchaperoned party in Storrs over the weekend, where all the cool kids had gathered and founded cliques that would endure through much of high school. I wouldn't have been invited even if I had been in town, nor would my parents have permitted me to attend, but the fact that so much was said to have happened—one couple was rumored to have "gone all the way," or most of the way, anyway—made me feel more alienated than ever. When I returned to Storrs, the man who ran the record store offered me a handshake and congratulations, and I was interviewed by the *Hartford Courant*. But my classmates were notably silent—on to other things, less and less interested in my films, tired of my domineering ways, sudden rudeness, and imperial intellectual arrogance. I knew no other way to behave, and I reflected miserably that I was probably going to be famous someday but that I was going to be alone.

Accepting the inevitable and looking for guidance, I fixated on the lives of accomplished loners—Bobby Fischer, Glenn Gould, Howard Hughes, J. D. Salinger—and I read everything that I could find about them. They were all greatly gifted men who seemed to share some of my paralysis but had also managed to make the world accept and acclaim them on their terms. That was my best hope, and I studied their examples. The hidden Hughes in particular fascinated me, even though I didn't have much interest in his work, with the sole exception of his creation of a special bra for Jane Russell, who had been a heroine ever since I had watched her, resplendent in rawhide, beat up a villain in *The Paleface*.

Prodigies have a tough time of things. I remember coming across one of Robert Ripley's grislier *Believe It or Not* sketches. "Boy Dies of Old Age at Seven!!" the headline read and, in the best Ripley manner, a few terse sentences, augmented by exclamation points, told of a child whose metabolism was so rapid that he learned to read at the age of two, grew a full beard at four, and withered away and died before his eighth birthday. The boy in the drawing bore a resemblance to the exhausted sage in a thousand New Year's editorial cartoons: spent and wizened, all but shut down, he yet peered at the reader through the eyes of a child.

I probably haven't seen that picture in thirty years, but I've thought about it often and at some length, and I suspect that most prodigies will respond to the image, for they, too, are simultaneously young and old. "Baby's brain and an old man's heart," began the lyrics to a popular hit of the early 1970s. Choose your own contradictions: the fingers of a master pianist on a scared little girl; an inarticulate shyness hiding the mathematical acuity of a calculator; profound artistic sensitivity that coexists with a remote, disengaged personality.

I'm grateful to David Hoffman for making *A Day with Timmy Page* and capturing part of my childhood for posterity so deftly and with such obvious affection. But I can't watch the film with much pleasure anymore, because I don't particularly like its central character. Not merely because I was rattling off all sorts of breezy critical judgments of films I hadn't seen (it would be another decade before I attended a screening of Griffith's *Intolerance,* one of the movies I had claimed to "adore"), nor because I was parroting *Classics of the Silent Screen* wholesale, passing off its philosophies as my own. These are minor inauthenticities, familiar to anyone who has ever attended a singles event, a faculty party, or any gathering on Manhattan Island.

No, what I really object to is my cavalier dismissal of my leading lady, whose name was then Anne Beddow. At one point in the film, I wonder out loud why I had brought her into the company in the first place, as though I really didn't think she was very good but, hey, you take what you can get, right? Wrong. Not only was this an ungracious way to treat someone who had been my true friend for almost five years at that point (and has remained my friend for another forty since); it was a complete and total misrepresentation of my feelings for Annie, which had by then blossomed into a mixture of idealization, hero worship, and wracking physical desire, all of which I was so determined to keep hidden that I sent out disinformation.

Annie was beautiful, freckled, long-legged, tall, and strong; she could do pretty much anything the boys could do, and usually better. She was also enormous fun, with none of the remove and frail fussiness that was expected of "young ladies" in those pre-feminist days. Her laughter was mischievous and wholehearted; she was a genuine pal, as well as my deep and secret crush.

I had always been attracted to tomboys, who seemed so confident and assured in worlds that were not my own. The first of these, when I was about seven years old, was Joan of Arc. I had a Landmark Book and a Classics Illustrated comic about her; I even managed to make it through Mark Twain's decidedly idiosyncratic biography, which may be the dullest thing he ever wrote. And I wasn't interested in the Maid of Orleans because she was a saint or because she saw holy visions or anything so noble as that. No, I loved her as a physical warrior, a woman who was out there clanking swords and charging fearlessly into battle, and I'd feel funny in my pants when I thought of her.

Joan of Arc would be followed by Wonder Woman, Batgirl, and Emma Peel (*The Avengers*) in my roster of early heroines. This response to powerful women—not at all in keeping with accepted male norms in the 1960s (although somebody must have had fun fashioning those gloriously kinky scenes in *The Avengers*)—caused me no small degree of embarrassment. I've analyzed it in ponderous detail, trying on all sorts of ideas, wondering whether it was my own physical awkwardness searching for its biological complement. Maybe it was yin in search of yang. Maybe my fear of annihilation made me yearn for an invulnerable rescuer.

Or maybe I just liked strong girls. Stranger things have happened.

It was never difficult for me to articulate feelings about anything impersonal. I never ran short of opinions, well founded or otherwise. But deeper emotions reduced me to aching silence, especially when I feared that I would be exposed, misunderstood, or ridiculed. And so I empathized with Rostand's Cyrano (a serious rival to Ferdinand the Bull in my private pantheon of literary heroes), daring and witty on the surface but too terrified to utter crucial words to the woman he loved.

Part of this hesitance had to do with an omnipresent horror of losing control, a fear of uncorking my own intensity of feeling, even unto violence. Once, when I was about five, the three of us were left with a horrible woman named Mrs. Conlon while my parents went to Washington for a week. She was truly sadistic, and her way of punishing me was to grab my nipples and twist them violently. In the middle of her interminable stay, I was climbing up on a stepladder that reached to the top of the refrigerator when I came across an ice pick; I threw it as hard as I could at the table where Mrs. Conlon was reading, a few feet away. And it didn't stick into the wood and quiver or anything as dramatic as that, but it certainly got her attention. "Do you want to *kill* me?" she screamed. I realized that I *had* wanted to kill her—sort of (my aim was definitely at the table, not at her back or her head)—and I was as alarmed by my action as she was, frightened into passivity.

And so it was with sex. I was thirteen and wrestling with a girl I'd met on a family trip to California. She was holding me down, smiling confidently, with what seemed to me a coolly exquisite ease, a distinctly *female* strength, and all of a sudden I climaxed, just like that. But there was nothing ecstatic about it: it was a weird, seismic, messy, and unexplained spasm that didn't really feel very good, not that first time. Perhaps I wasn't biologically ready yet. In any event, I had nobody to talk to about this: I knew that my mother would be horrified, and I feared that my father might want to write it up. Thereafter I found myself under enormous sexual tension, which I released every few weeks, always with a sense of grim and painful duty. It was at least a year before I relaxed and began to spend as many blissful hours in the bathroom as any ordinary teenager.

I remember my fourteenth year as the best since early childhood. I was learning to control my outbursts; my love of music was deepening; puberty had advanced far enough so that I was at least a little comfortable with it. It was a strange and interesting time at UConn—the nadir of the Vietnam War and the apex, to that date, of local activism. One Saturday morning, the Students for a Democratic Society took over Gulley Hall, then the campus's main office.

I heard about the rebellion on the local news, and I walked across campus to join several of my friends inside, not because of any incipient radicalism but out of purest curiosity. Gulley Hall seemed to have been invaded by visitors from another planet—playing guitars, smoking pot, talking about revolution, and all of this in Storrs!

In general, though, I was happier in the company of older people, some of whom were quite elderly indeed. Kate Lamson, who lived alone about a block from our house, was in her eighties and had been in Storrs most of her life. We'd sit in her violet-scented living room for hours at a time and talk about what UConn had been like half a century earlier. She could remember the day, in 1914, that Gold Hall burned down—the smoke, the bells, the shouting— and I was entranced, because I had a photograph of the original campus and knew what the dormitory had looked like. She recognized the names of my actors and singers, and had seen some of the films I'd read about, including Theda Bara's *Cleopatra*, of which, I knew, no print had survived. She would give me candy and tell me what a well-mannered young man I was, at a time when I badly needed reminding.

And then there was Harry Hannah, who was still shoveling his walkway on Route 44A at the age of ninety-five, and lived to become the oldest person in Connecticut. As the *Willimantic Chronicle* put it when he died at 110:

> Harry Hannah was born three years after
> Abraham Lincoln was shot, during the
> presidency of Andrew Johnson. There were

35 million people in the 37 states of the union. The telephone was invented when he was 10. Automobiles were not in popular use until he was nearly 50. One of his fondest memories was seeing the electric lights go on in New York in 1879. "Throngs of people came out that night, wandering up and down Broadway, marveling at so much light."

Even then, I understood that Mrs. Lamson and Mr. Hannah were precious and perishable, and I treated them with the utmost delicacy. In return, they were very kind to me and, as I grow older, I realize that they were probably astounded to find somebody who was still so interested in them, as they sat alone in their houses, after so much had been lost or taken away.

I modeled a character on Mrs. Lamson, in a fanciful 2,500-word story that I wrote in a single evening, typing it out on my father's gray, oversized IBM electric:

Nobody knew why the rain had not stopped. The weather report had said four in ten for light showers in the early morning. But here it was: 5 o'clock. And it was pouring.

There was nothing to stop Lady Lieg from leaving the library. She had all the equipment, a fold-up umbrella, galoshes, etcetera and so on. But there was this book on Alla Nazimova that just begged to be checked out. How could she resist it?

How indeed? In no way am I making a case that I possessed any innate talent for fiction (although it took a certain prescience to hypothesize a biography of the actress, director, and eventual gay icon Nazimova some thirty years before Gavin Lambert's volume was published). But, amid the usual obfuscating data, there are flashes of verisimilitude and understanding. By then, I had begun to trace in literature some emotional pathways that would fulfill me infinitely more than the road map of a Connecticut town or a list of names and dates from the back of an old recording.

But the book that helped pull me into the human race was Emily Post's *Etiquette,* which I had picked up in a moment of early-teen scorn, fully intending to mock what I was sure would be justification of bourgeois rules and regulations. Instead, Post explained the world to me. *Etiquette* offered clearly stated reasons for gallantry, gentility, and scrupulousness—reasons that I could understand, respect, and implement. It suggested ways to inaugurate conversations without launching into a lecture, reminded me of the importance of listening as well as speaking, and convinced me that manners, properly understood, existed to make other people feel comfortable, rather than (as I had suspected) to demonstrate the practitioner's social superiority. My confusion and ferocity began to be disciplined into courtesy; I reveled in Post's guidance and absorbed her lessons. And, typically, I took them too far. To this day, I would never dream of addressing a teenage busboy in a small-town diner as anything other than "sir."

I found Emily Post among my mother's paperbacks, but

most of the books I read came from the UConn library, where I was always made to feel at home, even in high rabbit's-foot regalia. Every room held treasures, but my favorite spot was the listening station at the Music Library, where, one blessed afternoon, I put on bulbous headphones that made me look like Mickey Mouse and heard the prelude to *Das Rheingold* for the first time.

The word that year was *psychedelic,* and I had only a vague idea of what it meant, although I had gleaned that *Sgt. Pepper's Lonely Hearts Club Band,* brightly colored Peter Max posters, mystical novels by Hermann Hesse, and the whole city of San Francisco were said to be awash in this new and magical quality. And then Wagner's depiction of the River Rhine started to play and a flowering drone filled my head; time was suspended, and I was transported.

Much has been made of Wagner's harmonic restlessness—of the way that a work such as *Tristan und Isolde* led inexorably to the so-called atonality of Arnold Schoenberg and his disciples. But what astonished me in *Das Rheingold,* although I couldn't have stated it then, was the opposite quality: the opera's unprecedented harmonic *stasis,* the manner in which it explored the churning inner life of sustained chords, from the three amazing minutes of E-flat major that set the score in motion through the affirmation of the Gods, Valhalla, and eternal D-flat major at the end. This was music that one could dwell in, a sort of sonic weather. I loved its resistance to change, its protracted unfolding, its mantric sense of perpetual return.

Meanwhile, I was discovering some of the same qualities in Indian raga and in the early music of Steve Reich and Terry Riley, which was reiterative and rhythmical and near-hypnotic, and I lost myself in it. (In my own idiosyncratic version of paradise, Reich's *Music for Mallet Instruments, Voices and Organ* would always be playing in one Elysian pasture or another.) I proudly announced that I had grown to like modern jazz, which was already vaguely respectable in classical circles, but I secretly preferred the streamlined, claustrophobic steadiness of hard rock, which wasn't. My curiosity extended to other fields. I read Camus's *The Plague* and was doing my best to crack Joyce's *Ulysses*. There was a terrific Friday-night film series at UConn where I saw *Jules and Jim, The Battleship Potemkin,* and a lot of pre- and post–*Wild Strawberries* Bergman for the first time, regularly leaving the theater stirred to my soul.

So there I was—a self-defined conservative individualist with mostly lefty, arty companions and an unusual openness to contemporary creative expression. All in all, I was more comfortable with myself than I had ever been, and I sometimes wonder what might have happened to me if we had stayed in Storrs and I had been able to continue growing up with the people I knew.

FIVE

Even more disheveled than usual in the Campo
Alegre school pageant. Caracas, 1969.

A year is forever when you're young, and the longest year
of my life was spent with my family in Caracas, Venezuela,
starting in the summer of 1969. It was my father's sabbatical, a free semester granted to professors every seven years
which he managed to extend from June to June. He had
been hired by the Ford Foundation to work with the Minister of Education in the slums of the city and, whether we
liked it or not, we were all going with him.

On June 20, 1969, we boarded the *Santa Paula,* one of
two flagships of the Grace Line, at New York's Houston
Street pier, and sailed at midnight. This was my only experience with an ocean liner—those glorious dinosaurs were

already disappearing from the scene—and I took to it immediately, hunting down private decks where I could compose and write and gaze out poetically at the sea, hitherto experienced only from the confines of a beach. I ate good food (not only my first Lobster Thermidor but my first lobster of any sort, and there were buffets full of them) and stayed up as late as I wanted in the ship's bar, observing how silly adults could be once they'd had a few drinks. I decided that I liked luxury, but I also enjoyed the enforced monotony of the days—the sense that we were going to be on the boat for a week, so that we'd best settle down, adjust our systems, and get used to it, as though we were characters in a long opera.

Because Caracas is three thousand feet above the Caribbean Sea, we docked at the port of La Guaira, which would be the site of an appalling catastrophe decades later after torrential rains triggered a mudslide that buried the four-hundred-year-old city and killed at least thirty thousand people in a single night. Back in 1969, La Guaira was considered steamy, crowded, and a place to be escaped as quickly as possible; I now wish I had stored more memories of this latter-day Pompeii. As our cab climbed into the mountains toward Caracas on the most vertiginous and treacherously winding road I could imagine, I was both thrilled and terrified at the realization that the red needle on the driver's speedometer rarely dropped below a hundred. Only later would it dawn on me that Venezuelan cars count in kilometers.

Caracas was then a city of a little more than two million—fierce, noisy, friendly, fast-paced, chaotic, and clotted with automobiles and buses that puffed pestilential clouds of blackest smoke toward the sky. In addition to the native Venezuelans (some 70 percent of whom were of mixed race, with the rest divided among white, black, and Indian), the city was filled with immigrants—a sizable Jewish community that had fled Hitler in the 1930s and more than a few Italians and Germans who had found it expedient to leave their own countries at the end of World War II. In Caracas, it was pretty much agreed that whatever might or might not have happened in the Old World was over and the only clash of cultures that was obvious to me was the significant one between those who had money and those who did not.

Downtown was dirty and poor, and rarely visited by Americans unless there was official business to attend to or a Sunday-morning concert at the Teatro Municipal. The eastern suburbs—Altamira, Chacao, Las Mercedes, and the newly developed Prados del Este—were wealthy, private, and meticulously kept. All Caracas met on an eternally crowded street called the Sabana Grande: there were bookstores and restaurants with impossibly fresh fruit and outdoor tables where conversations and chess games would continue late into the night, where smiling children would offer to sell you newspapers (a musical "MOON-doe!"—for *El Mundo*—was their evening cry) or shine your shoes for the price of a twenty-two-cent bolivar.

We lived in La Florida, one of the original suburbs, which was considered a little too close to the center of Caracas to be truly fashionable. It was also integrated— mansions and shingle-board shacks might share the same block. Storrs was virtually all white in those days, and I fear that I arrived in Caracas something of a bigot, a deplorable state that lasted until I actually met a couple of black people. By the end of the year, I was immersed in Afro-Caribbean culture, especially the wild, tranced salsa music that blasted from pulsating speakers in the corners of cantinas, which makes me happy to this day. I also learned that I loved cities, and I'm still more comfortable in any sort of urban environment, however unfashionable—Detroit, St. Louis, Cleveland, even Atlantic City—than I am in the poshest depopulated enclaves. Somewhere Charles Baudelaire wrote about the joys of taking a bath in crowds, and I continue to find deep exhilaration in moving anonymously through unfamiliar throngs.

Caracas has had a miserable press in recent years. I've revisited five times, both under center-right presidents and under the unpredictable leftist Hugo Chávez, and I confess that I don't think the basic feel of the city has changed very much, not yet anyway. It remains a crowded, exuberant, ill-governed madhouse—profoundly stimulating and wildly exasperating—that one either loves or loathes. To be sure, Sabana Grande is now run-down, and once-tony neighborhoods such as Candelaria, San Bernardino, and even parts of La Florida are considered dangerous after dark. But there have been advancements, too—notably a safe, fast, clean, and reliable subway system that has reduced traffic and improved the air quality. Music of all kinds resounds throughout Caracas, and it is one of my favorite places to fill my stomach, from the churros and arepas sold on the street to steak and Peking duck. The very thought of an impending visit makes me feel younger, as though that long-discredited form of rejuvenation, bull's glands, had been injected into my system and proven effective after all.

Yet the sabbatical was a terrible year for me to live through. I had begun to define myself in Storrs—as an eccentric, buttoned-up, oblivious kid who was known and tolerated as such, and sometimes even loved. I was accustomed to my role as loyal opposition in a bohemian crowd that took almost everything with a dose of skepticism. And now I was in a very different, decidedly anti-bohemian world—a private Venezuelan American school, filled with the wealthy and complacent children of oil magnates, ambassadors, and military officers stationed in a foreign playground.

The school was called Escuela Campo Alegre, and I promptly dubbed it "Concentration Campo." What clothes you wore were judged extremely important, as were your shoes, and I simply didn't get any of it, for I'd always thought of clothes mostly as something to cover the body and shoes as something to protect the feet. I crossed my legs above the knee on my first day of class and was immediately labeled a "faggot," a word I did not understand, although there was no mistaking its hostile intention.

Expatriate politics tilted far right of center—I thought it terribly strange that all these ultra-Americanists had chosen to leave home and live in Venezuela—and there was a general contempt for "Vens" that was expressed regularly and noisily by my fellow students. The animosity was sometimes reciprocated: eleven years earlier, Vice President

Richard Nixon's car had been attacked in Caracas, and there were still regular anti-U.S. protests at the Universidad, during which all Campo Alegre students were sent home and ordered to stay there. It was possible to take unintended amusement from a long-standing advertisement in the *Daily Journal,* the city's English-language newspaper, which boasted that a venerable hotel was located "a stone's throw from the American embassy."

Yet I liked the Venezuelans I met more than I did most of my fellow Americans, who were intolerant of my quirks and my general sloppiness. But my real trouble was with Campo's principal, Mr. Price, a martinet who went into a rage whenever he saw my shirttail out, as it inevitably was. Once, I had failed to get a proper hall pass to go to the bathroom, and Mr. Price shoved me up against the wall and screamed in my face. He thought I was flaunting my contempt for everything he stood for; in reality, I was trying very hard to conceal it.

I rebelled and adopted a persona that I would maintain and embellish during the next five years. Suddenly I went all over to the counterculture. I brought a volume of Karl Marx to school; this was noted and I was instructed never to repeat the offense. (I knew that the choice would attract attention, and probably started every conversation that day with "Hey, look at me—I'm reading Karl Marx, who is a Communist and hates America!" or something equally subtle.) I learned all the Venezuelan swear words and used them with alacrity. I bought a pack of cigarettes and taught myself to inhale. I drank a beer on Sabana Grande. And I decided that it was time to try marijuana.

It would have happened anyway. Most of my Storrs pals had been smoking pot for months or even a couple of years; a number of them had already outgrown it. The weed grew wild in Venezuela; you could be arrested for possessing some of it in a plastic bag, but not for having the plants on your property unless there was evidence of cultivation. There was just too much marijuana around; any police action would have been a little like trying to ban ivy from the English countryside.

I decided to prove to my classmates that I was far, far hipper than they could ever be. I started to laugh like Dennis Hopper in *Easy Rider,* which I thought was a perfectly dreadful film, but Hopper's wasted giggling seemed to have the ring of authenticity and I borrowed it. I read *Rolling Stone* magazine and Timothy Leary, immersed myself in the two mescaline-inspired essays by Aldous Huxley, and bragged of my supposed psychedelic adventures to anyone who would listen. The way I stared into space and never comprehended questions from my teachers? Why, I was *stoned,* you fools—couldn't you tell?

Sooner or later I had to prove myself, of course, and I was invited out for a Saturday of smoke. Two of our foursome freely admitted that they'd never tried pot before; neither had I, but nobody was going to learn that. We listened to some new, not very good albums—*The Soft Parade, Three Dog Night Captured Live at the Forum,* and the *Easy Rider* soundtrack—and inhaled all day, to disappointing effect. Eventually we taxied over to the house of one of the nicest girls in our class, Nancy Bruggemeyer, where a sedate and decidedly drug-free party was in progress. There, about twenty of us were lazing on her back lawn when somebody threw a sneaker over my head. And suddenly it looked like the spacecraft in *2001: A Space Odyssey,* all aglow, gliding grandly and timelessly across the cosmos . . .

I smoked pot only once more during my stay in Caracas, but I spoke about it incessantly and with assumed authority, and I began to attract the notice I craved, not only from students but from parents, teachers, and administrators as well. I had determined that I wasn't going to be little classical-piano-film-nerd Timmy Page ever again but an intrepid explorer of inner space, a wise hipster who knew all the answers. And what better way to prove my maturity, savoir faire, and revolutionary credentials than to scribble "FUCK PRICE!" on the wall of the boys' room while I was there on business one morning?

The administration pounced, and I quickly confessed. My penance was to scrub down every seat in the open-air auditorium. This ate up my recess time, but I grew to like the calm regularity of the task. A lovely girl named Susan— the lone reason I could ever muster to attend the United Christian Church—was angry about what had happened to me and proceeded to commit a copy-cat crime. She was far more delicate than I had been ("Price is a nut!"), but the deed was done and I was blamed for it and suspended for a week.

As I went to clear out my books for home study, I was summoned into a classroom by Mrs. Castello, my math teacher, and one of her colleagues at the school, Mr.

Hutchinson, who taught English. They were both British and shared the good, sharp sense of humor endemic to their background, as well as an affection for me, even though I was one of their poorer students. I swore that I hadn't written this new graffito, and they assured me such a calumny had never crossed their minds. "Oh no, Tim—your use of language is much more vivid than that," Mrs. Castello said, and started laughing. "Next time, use more than four letters when you insult Price," Mr. Hutchinson added. "That way, he won't be able to read them." By then, I was laughing, too. It was the first time I had ever heard one adult admit that another might be an idiot—most of the time, they kept strict solidarity—and I was amazed and relieved to know that I hadn't disgraced myself with all the grown-ups at Campo.

Susan, a noble soul, admitted what she had done first thing Monday morning, but my suspension remained in effect. The official excuse was that I had written a third slur against Mr. Price in some other, unspecified spot. I hadn't.

Stung by this blatantly unfair treatment, my father wrote a four-thousand-word letter of formal protest to the school superintendent, a certain Roland Roth. I would not uncover this document, excerpted below, for another nine years, when my parents were preparing to move away from Storrs and I was given charge of packing my father's files:

> Our own position, with Tim and with Mr.
> Price, has been complete support for authority.
> And it remains so today. From our point of
> view, it is *Tim* who must change. He must be

far more subordinate, more subservient to
authority, more attentive to instructions, more
abiding by rules. I have never seen any rash of
such graffiti directed at a principal in my own
experience as teacher or as educator. I have no
sympathy with those who carry it on. I think it
deserves strict repression and punishment. The
fact that my own son Tim once participated
in it is a source of lasting embarrassment,
amazement and shame. He is *still* being
punished for it at home. We are also *not*
showing him this letter or giving him sympathy
or verbal support in our conversations with
him.

All this I remembered—the month after my suspension
was probably the most miserable period of my childhood—
but my father went on, and I sensed his love flooding off
the paper:

As superintendent, you of course know very
little about Tim, and that filtered, as we have
said, through the very narrow window of
official report and random incident. But he is a
splendid, gifted, creative, productive and
(within his special fields) extremely
hardworking boy.
He was reading long before he entered
kindergarten and has long measured at the
superior-adult scale in vocabulary. This verbal

ability is of course part of what you described as a "Big Mouth" with Tim. He *is* extremely skillful in verbal subtleties and logical permutations—in a word, he is highly "articulate" and when this combines with a critical attitude toward authority it can be very exasperating, whether the authority is parent, teacher, or principal.

This extreme verbal ability has been noticed in a number of ways. Perhaps you would like to see a 17-minute professional film, made by a free-lance photographer about Tim, which has won several national and international prizes, has been exhibited at the New York Film Festival and is now commercially circulated by McGraw Hill. It is called, of all titles, "A Day With Timmy Page" and shows the then-12-year-old Tim as a backyard movie producer, organizing a film and theorizing about film history. There wasn't a word of scripting: this was pure creative talent, Tim's and the photographer's.

His filmmaking still goes on and grows in depth (he has made perhaps his best film here). But filmmaking is almost trivial beside the dominating intellectual and aesthetic passion of his life—which is music. You cannot *begin* to understand Tim without understanding the obsessive and profound nature of this passion. This also began at a very early age—he insisted on playing classic records repeatedly when he was 24 months old. Today, the biggest "punishment" we could give him is to keep him from playing the piano—not systematically, not always exactly what his teacher (Mrs. Harriet Serr) has assigned, but what is currently most puzzling or exciting to him. But more than playing, he takes an obsessive interest in musical history, styles, people, movements, changes. Unless you have first-hand experience with him in this regard and are in a position to know what he is talking about, it is very difficult to believe the depth of his knowledge and the rapidity with which it is developing at this very moment—and has been developing more and more, each year.

If we can extrapolate his present development into the future—and most especially if his understanding of modern trends continues to mature—he will make a major contribution to some creative field closely related to music.

But the negative traits are obvious in a school setting. Tim is bored by many classes and inclined to day dream. He is often inept at getting along with both teachers and students. He has never taken routine assignments seriously and his grades (unlike his objective achievement scores) are a shambles as a result. He gets B's, C's, and D's, with an occasional F.

This failure worries him terribly, especially just
before grade time and just after, but it has not
yet led him to join the rest of the family in the
honors category. He catches hell at school and
at home for this failure, and the kind of
attitude toward responsibility which it
represents. We must add, however, the
following: both his teachers and parents are
troubled by this so-called "underachievement."
The fact is that Tim *is* getting well-educated
both at school and at home, except for the
reactions of the teachers, which are the
"grades." That is to say, on any measure of
general achievement in an area (aside from just
what a teacher assigned for a given day) he will
appear objectively well-informed, well beyond
his years and, in his special areas, well beyond
the typical university graduate. This is not
made to excuse him (and we keep the pressure
on) but just to point out a fact: that as
educators we sometimes confuse our courses
with the main heritage of Western culture. We
shouldn't.

I wept when I came across this letter, which I continue to
regard as a magnificent defense, the most searching and
sympathetic description of my condition ever offered up to
that time—and from the person I had begun to consider as
my nemesis! How I wish my father had been able to communicate such tender emotions to me then, for throughout

most of the 1970s I perceived only his harshness and for several lost years we barely spoke to each other.

The letter failed to move the authorities, however, and steps were taken to turn suspension into expulsion. Campo Alegre had a part-time therapist, referred to grandly as "La Señora Dottora Vega," and she evinced a new and hitherto unimaginable interest in me once I resumed classes. She called me into her office and won my trust with the first display of official kindness I'd received from the school. She explained that our talks would be "confidential," and I now knew what the word meant. And so, a guileless and lonely chatterbox, I went on at great length about myself— my frustrations, my aspirations, my fears, my music, *the names of the other children who were smoking pot at Campo Alegre.* . . .

Of course, La Señora Dottora Vega was a spy. Everything I told her went directly to Price and Roth, and a roundup of erring students followed directly. My new friends were specifically informed that it was I who had ratted them out, an unbelievably cruel and unnecessary twist of the knife. Two boys were eventually disciplined—none, as my father noted with a rare and commendable touch of radical outrage, with "strong ties to or support from the Venezuelan-American power elite"—and I was asked to leave.

I spent my last month in Caracas at home, as we prepared for our return to Connecticut. I was determined to come back Cool. I didn't have the physical capacity to be a jock; my grades were too poor for me to fit in with the future Ivy Leaguers; I had none of the comfortable composure necessary to be a class leader—and, in fact, I really wasn't interested in most of these people. But I might just fit in with the newly minted group of hippies—or "freaks," as they more generally called themselves, "hippie" having joined "groovy" and "gage" and "Frisco" as one of those media buzzwords that no self-respecting member of the counterculture would ever utter.

Mainly, I wanted to impress Annie, so I wrote her a letter in big, black Magic Marker scrawls, entirely with capital letters that spread out over the sixteen pages of a complete edition of the *Daily Journal,* which I used as stationery, boasting of my suspension and my new politics and how much longer my hair had grown. I suspect this came across as unsettling and more than a little crazed, rather than the dynamic and romantic credo I had planned—the letter had some of the wired, irrational energy of a ransom note—but she has held on to it for almost four decades, a souvenir of strange times.

SIX

Bald fifteen-year-old acidhead. Storrs, 1970.

I returned to the United States on June 12, 1970, eight days short of a year after I had left. Much had changed. Four students at Kent State University had been shot and killed six weeks earlier and there had been rioting on campuses from coast to coast for much of the spring, culminating in Storrs with a mercifully bloodless bombing of the faculty club. William F. Buckley, Jr., published a nationally syndicated column equating UConn with the University of Havana. Marijuana was everywhere—passed around openly in the College Theater during showings of *2001: A Space Odyssey* and the newly re-released *Fantasia*—and LSD was increasingly common. Hitchhiking, out of fashion for much of the 1960s, had made a comeback, although the 1969 murder of a UConn student, Paget Weatherly, just off campus, had shocked the community and we were warned against the practice. My group didn't listen; we couldn't afford to listen, because there was no other way to get around town.

I had heard that Annie had a boyfriend, but hoped I might still win her over until I met him. Paul was gigantic—at least twice as wide as I was and all muscle. He was also three years older, had a full black beard, wore a leather jacket, rode a motorcycle, and exuded a confident and aggressive manliness that I couldn't begin to emulate. It was as though I'd been introduced to a member of a different species, and I had never felt skinnier or more awkward. But Annie greeted me joyfully, and we continued a serene and unbroken lifelong friendship. To this day, few things make me happier than the chime of her laughter, especially when something that I've said is its cause.

My other pre-Caracas friends, with college looming a couple of years off, were rather put out by my new wildman persona and many of them broke off contact, either for a while or forever. I joined a new crowd that summer—a group of amiable, untethered maniacs who spent most of their time hanging around the University of Connecticut Student Union, smoking cigarettes and drinking vanilla Cokes at the soda fountain. They bragged incessantly of the drugs they took, the political circles in which they were welcomed, and—especially—the women with whom they had slept. One of them told me that he had bedded eleven different girls in a single twenty-four-hour period and, credulous soul, I not only believed his every word but imagined that such an Olympian accomplishment would have been great fun.

July 4, 1970, was just another day at the Student Union—duller than most, because the UConn students were gone, the shops in Storrs were closed, and most of our friends were out of town for the holiday. I was fifteen and I'd never kissed a girl—never, in fact, even held a girl's hand except in dreaded, bruising games of Red Rover at summer camp. But I noticed that there was this vastly mature eighteen-year-old *woman* watching me across the lobby, and all I knew about her was that she was the older sister of one of Betsy's friends and very pretty. She was wearing a minidress that looked as though it had been confected from fake leopard fur, and I stole as many would-be-surreptitious glances at her legs as I could. Somehow, we were introduced—we probably smoked some pot together—and then we found ourselves alone in a stranger's apartment in an off-campus building called Storrs Manor. I still wasn't sure of her first name, but she sat extremely close beside me on an otherwise empty couch and I finally decided, by the process of elimination, that something had to be going on, that there simply wasn't any other logical explanation for her immediate physical proximity.

And so I made my move, with a nervous utterance that can still make me blush:

"Do you feel like some *love* tonight?"

She grinned at me through her granny glasses, with as much amusement as ardor. "Maybe," she whispered coyly, after what seemed forever.

I gulped and stared at the ground—it couldn't be this simple, could it?

"Uh . . . f-from *me*?"

I followed her into a bedroom. There, in a matter of three seconds, she slipped out of her sandals and lifted her dress over her head, revealing both her matching fake-leopard-skin bikini panties and her big bare breasts, just like in the movies and the magazines. What on earth was I supposed to do with *those*? I wondered. I was petrified, but she was patient and tender, we managed some sort of coupling, and I felt thrilled and a little alarmed by the heightened intensity of the explosion when it happened.

When I arrived the next day, I proudly told my Student Union pals of my accomplishment, but I had badly misgauged their reaction.

"You did *what*? With *her*? BWAHAHAHAHAHA!!!" And suddenly they were up in the classrooms above the lobby, scrawling "Tim Page fucked X—— X——!" on all the blackboards throughout the building, yelling it down the halls, laughing hysterically and slapping their legs, a total nightmare.

Of course, I learned later that they were nasty little virgins, steamed up because I'd done something that they'd only talked about. Still, the fact remains that I was so embarrassed that I walked past my first lover the following day and didn't even look at her. Now, I know it was all supposed to be "free love," with no hassles or commitments (so we told ourselves), and yes, I was very young, but my behavior was ungallant in the extreme and this is one more person to whom I've long owed an apology.

It was another year before I nearly had sex again. Our group had found an abandoned storm cellar way out in the woods off Route 44, and we had converted it into a clubhouse, going so far as to find a beat-up old couch to furnish it. The cellar was a breeding ground for mosquito hawks, which look like the largest and most frightening bloodsuckers imaginable but in fact ignore human beings and feast on standard-issue mosquitoes. Their guardianship was a blessing on wet, buggy New England nights.

So there we were. The young woman with whom I was sharing a six-pack had bought into the hippie mythos bigtime. "I don't understand why people don't just sit around and *ball*," she said meaningfully, "ball" being that summer's word of choice. "You know, just get up in the morning and call up a friend and get together and *ball*. Wouldn't that be a wonderful world, just *balling* everybody all the time?"

Once again, my superbly tuned radar didn't let me down. "Well, um, maybe that's what *we* should do!" I ventured brightly. We kissed and took off our clothes in the darkness and professed our desire for each other, and she gave me a gigantic hickey on the end of my chin that would still be purple three days later. And then, just as things were beginning to get serious, her bravado disappeared. She moaned, admitted that this would be her first time, and asked me if I'd still feel the same way tomorrow.

I thought about that for a second. "I have absolutely no idea," I replied honestly.

Wrong answer. We parted as friends.

It is strange for veterans of the so-called sexual revolution to learn about younger generations, who sound much more sophisticated than we were, if no less reckless. I recently read of a high school survey in which roughly eighty percent of the graduating seniors were said to have had oral sex and fifty percent had had intercourse. Setting aside moral judgments and personal preferences for a second (can that still be done?), my guess is that the percentages would have been reversed in the early 1970s. After all, oral sex demands some concentrated physical intimacy with your partner; we merely unzipped, wriggled nervously, and zipped up again, which required no real closeness at all. Most boys my age knew nothing about the female anatomy, and the most accessible studies we had, the nudes in *Playboy*, weren't even permitted to possess genitalia until 1970.

I was never suited for promiscuity, although I certainly tried my best. I now realize that if I had fewer encounters than most of my friends it was by choice, but I didn't see it that way at the time, when it seemed that life was one big orgy that I was just managing to miss. My seduction technique was to go to a party and sit down and talk with my female buddies—about their innermost feelings, their problems with their parents, the Philosophies of Sisterhood—and, to my surprise, their eyes would start to glaze. Then some tough guy, all testosterone and machismo, would burst into the room, grunt, and carry them off. Given both permission and impetus to shed their inhibitions, they disappeared into the back room. "Bye, Tim!" they would call out with delighted relief, for they were just as shy and new at this as I was.

My discomfort must have shown through, because I managed to handily desex any possible matchups. There was one especially lovely girl, a violinist with a Botticelli face and rarefied elegance. I informed all of her friends about my crush and composed volumes of pimply poetry for her, but I never managed to say a word to her directly, although she gave me plenty of opportunity. How I ached as I watched her fall into a slow dance with Bobby Nichols—witnessed their frank and unashamed joy in the warmth of each other's arms—while I stood aside, snowman in a corner.

I grew convinced that my parentally enforced short hair was ruining my chances with women. Strange as it may seem, hair really mattered then—it was a badge of . . . well, *something,* anyway, if only a sort of prefabricated conformist rejection of prefabricated conformist values. The popular Broadway musical *Hair* had lyrics that were little more than a laundry list of no-no's but was influential nevertheless, and the best rock bands were scruffy to their shoulders, like most of my acquaintances. David Crosby wrote a pathetic song called "Almost Cut My Hair"—it was a major existential dilemma for him and for many others—and my friend Cory Crossgrove had hair so long that he could sit on it, something people were always telling him to do anyway.

When my father made it clear that the time for my first stateside haircut had arrived, I did not willingly acquiesce. I posed various arguments, pointing out how attractive long hair looked on writers we both admired. Oscar Wilde was no doubt an ill-chosen example, from my father's perspective—but what about Milton and Shakespeare? For that matter, w-what about *Jesus,* huh? It was all for naught, and I was told to get rid of my locks before nightfall.

Which was exactly what I did. Cory and Kevin Cawley stopped over and we took my father's clippers and shaved the middle of my head completely bald, leaving a little hair at both temples (a style quite similar to the way I wear it today, for a different reason). We had a hilarious, nihilistic time, and I wrapped up my shorn head and walked into Betsy's bedroom, where I let the towel drop and blurted out something along the lines of "Gee, this shampoo is *terrible*." She screamed and called my mother, who sighed and strongly urged me to finish the job before my father got home. And so we shaved my head bare, and then Cory and Kevin wrote graffiti—peace symbols, op art, "Stop Nixon!"—all over my scalp with multicolored Magic Markers, like so much war paint.

My father was shocked speechless by this apparition, and for once I felt truly sorry for him. After a prolonged, despairing silence, he shook his head and said, "I'll never ask you to do that again." My next haircut took place three years later and by then it hardly mattered.

I told everybody at school that I had shaved my head on an acid trip ("Snakes were growing out of my *brains, man!*"). However, as in Caracas, I babbled a whole lot more about drugs than I actually did them. I smoked pot hungrily for about two years, but I tried most of the "harder stuff" within six months of my return to the United States. Today, as a mostly respectable adult, it would be nice to pretend that I just outgrew this phase and decided, all by my lonesome, to obey the laws of the land and take better care of myself. But the fact of the matter was that drugs simply didn't much like me: stimulants made my heart palpitate and my hands quake, and even marijuana increasingly induced a rigid, solitary anxiety instead of the spacey contentedness it had provided at the outset.

LSD held a fascination, though. The drug, illegal for only four years then, had just enough science, mysticism, artistic cachet, and (let's face it) purest pretension associated with it to attract my attention. I had heard stories of how LSD permitted unhappy people to break through to a new peace—Huxley, the Beatles, and even Cary Grant had testified to this—and I thought it might provide that miracle cure I was seeking. I imagined that a trip would be like swallowing a movie or something—you'd sit back calmly and watch the hallucinations in your head as though they were taking place on a screen. I had no idea what sort of volcanic chaos I would be unleashing within what was already a delicate and disordered psyche.

My LSD trips were nightmarish, but at least they were interesting nightmares, especially when compared with the more predictable horrors associated with too much alcohol ("room spun . . . slept with wrong person . . . threw up"). Some editor ought to assemble an Old Fireside Book of Psychedelic Experience, interviewing acid-gulping graybeards before we drop off the planet. Michel Foucault reportedly took his first trip in the cold of a California desert night, listening to one of Karlheinz Stockhausen's electronic epics squawk from the speakers in a van. His friends came to him at dawn and found him awake in his sleeping bag, a wide grin on his skull. "I finally understand Malcolm Lowry's *Under the Volcano*," he said between shivers.

Storrs was dripping with LSD throughout the rainy fall

of 1970. Our high school was right on the UConn campus, and a freshman dorm unit called the Jungle, traditionally known for its beer parties and its intense overcrowding, briefly became the local pleasure dome. At the start of the school year, Jungle residents still took a few precautionary measures: towels might be placed under the door, and some incense might be lit to cover up the smell of whatever else was burning in the room. By semester break, the only reason to bother shutting the door at all was to keep others from crashing the ceaseless party or if you were going to have sex with somebody. Five years earlier, a male student might have had to see the dean if he was caught with a female in the room, even if the two were just studying. In an astonishingly short time, the barriers had come down.

I fashioned myself an LSD connoisseur, and the acid that most appealed to my fifteen-year-old palate was the mild "Sacrament of the Neo-American Church"—a tiny drop on white paper that was the lysergic equivalent of a couple of glasses of white wine on the rocks. A much stronger and more intense acid—a sort of psychedelic rotgut—was sold out of Belden Hall; this resembled a glob of mucilage atop a stamp-size snippet of green construction paper, it was probably cut with speed, and was certainly responsible for many an anxious evening across campus ("Were those *black widows* I saw crawling out of the television set?" "Of *course* not! Now, everything will be fine as long as you don't forget to *breathe*").

Then there was Orange Sunshine, a legendarily strong barrel-shaped pill similar to a chip off a chewable vitamin C tablet. Split one of these into quarters or even eighths and you'd have everybody stoned for a long time. I'd taken a tiny chunk in late summer and loved it, lying on my back with my head between stereo speakers while my "guide," who claimed to have taught a course in "LSD Psychotherapy" somewhere, played incessant songs like Dylan's "Sad-Eyed Lady of the Lowlands" and Phil Ochs's "When in Rome," both of which were new to me and neatly muddled my sense of time. This had been my very first trip, and I'd had such a good time that I knew the effects of a whole pill were bound to be paradisiacal.

One morning I took an entire tablet of Orange Sunshine and walked to school. It quickly became apparent that I couldn't stay in class—the elderly Miss Goyette was repeatedly dividing into any number of trolls—so I went to the nurse's office. This time, however, I couldn't quiet myself. I recall the sweaty palms, the deep bags under my eyes, the strange patterns of transient purple acne that appeared on my face when I looked in the mirror, an incessant need to urinate, and, increasingly, the sense that the cottage-cheese walls were pulsating, as though the Tell-Tale Heart itself had been concealed within.

It seemed a good idea to run away from school altogether, and at top speed, so I bade goodbye to the nurse and went over to the old UConn library, sitting in a room that looked as I'd always imagined a London gentleman's club might look—overstuffed chairs, oak paneling, and paintings, veddy veddy nice. But now the print on the magazine pages kept jumping out at me, random words quivering and italicized, and suddenly there was red-flame graffiti racing around the walls like the newswire at Times Square.

Most of this was too rapid-fire to be intelligible, but every now and then I could decipher a phrase—"Stinky loves Patsy," "Rats in the soup," "Nothing really matters," and other profundities.

I started to recite a little poem to myself:

> *I'm stoned.*
> *All a-lone.*
> *And STONED.*

But then the poem took control of me and I couldn't stop repeating it; the words reverberated around me, and my voice seemed to be rising higher and squeakier, as though I were inhaling helium from a gas mask. The strangeness increased, and finally I decided, once and for all, that it was time to venture outside again and make a last stand for reality. I lay down on the grass facing the rear of the Student Union, a sort of quad, closed my eyes, and tried to recover.

In those days, UConn had mysterious bells and whistles that sounded at different times during the course of the day; you could hear them all over campus. When the noon bell rang, I looked up and the buildings loomed large and menacing, as though I were trapped inside a fish-eye lens, and I sensed that something was about to go very wrong.

All at once, in strict time, like so many robots, a group of white men in formal suits exited a building on the left side of the Quad and a group of black workmen in white janitorial outfits walked out from one on the right. They walked purposefully toward each other, about twenty or thirty feet in front of me, and the sky was tick-tocking and the grass waved up and down, a vision from late van Gogh.

"Holy *shit*—it's the Civil War!" I gasped, and started to run. And run. When I was perhaps two miles away, I sat down to catch my breath. But then I looked up at the sky and realized that the sun was out. A famous story crossed what was left of my mind, about a group of LSD trippers who had gotten so wasted and stared so intently at the sun that they destroyed their eyes forever.

"Oh my God," I realized, horror-stricken. "The sun is going to melt my eyeballs."

It never occurred to me that I could simply choose not to look skyward—no, I was much too far gone for that. Light pierced from every direction—from the sky, the woods, the street—with that same sense of overexposure as when an optometrist dilates the pupils and prescribes dark glasses for the rest of the day. The world caught fire and I was sure that I could feel my eyes coming to a boil, so I ran up to a random split-level house and started to bang on the front door.

"Let me in!" I cried. "The sun is melting my eyeballs!"

A middle-aged woman, peeking through her window, saw a crazed, tearful young man with a shaved head hammering on her door and was understandably alarmed. "Who is that?"

"Let me in! *Please* let me in! The sun is melting my eyeballs!"

The door locked with a thud, and I slid down and began to whimper on the doorstep.

"Let me in . . . my eyeballs are melting, my eyeballs are melting."

Long silence. "Is that you, Timmy Page?"

The name sounded familiar.

"Timmy. It's Mrs. Gill. I bowl with your mother!"

Um.

"Does she know that you're here?"

Ummm . . .

Another long silence. Then, without ever opening the door (the Manson family was currently on trial in Los Angeles, and one couldn't be too careful), she called out and said, "Betty will be over in five minutes."

By now, I was slightly calmer—amazing how restorative remembering your name can be!—and I was sitting on Mrs. Gill's steps, peering down at all sorts of imagined activity on the ground. My mother sailed up Bundy Lane in her endless white 1967 Bonneville station wagon, a sleek monument to cheap gasoline, and I thought of Cinderella's coach and steeds. The electric window buzzed down, and she peered out with concern. At that precise moment, her face exploded into a squalling riot of hairy, tomato-colored vegetation, but I remembered my manners and addressed her formally.

"Mother, I'm sorry to have to tell you this, but I've just gone *totally* insane."

"Timmy, what is the matter with you? Have you taken drugs?"

And then, for the first time in several hours, I thought of the Orange Sunshine.

"Yes!" I shouted, and my voice resonated as though it were the highest, loudest chorus in Beethoven's *Missa Solemnis.* "Yes, I took drugs! That's right! I took acid! I'm *not* insane! I took *acid!*" And so on, for most of the ten-minute drive down to the Windham Memorial Hospital emergency ward, where a doctor rammed a needle into my rear end and I watched all the colors, graffiti, and demons wash away like icicles.

If you can believe it, I actually took LSD two or three more times before I stopped for good. After that, I became evangelically opposed to it and could grow quite agitated when the subject came up. Not everybody agreed with me; I remember the put-down I received from one snippy, trippy waitress at a local hangout. "I can understand why *you* don't take it," she said, with the tone of somebody who had just been handed a warm turd. "*You* clearly have no control over your own head." She was certainly right about that. I can well believe that LSD, administered in a carefully controlled environment under the supervision of sensitive and well-trained doctors, may yet prove to have some therapeutic value. But it remains the drug that scares me the most, for its consequences cannot be foreseen and I can now imagine fates far worse than death.

My friend K.B., a passionate tripper, refused to stop taking acid, although every experience was a fresh disaster that further disassociated him from the known world. After each new bummer, he would insist that if he could wangle himself just one more really *good* trip it would "fix" his head once and for all. He was obsessed with Jimi Hendrix,

then recently dead, who had appeared to him in a halluci-
nation and promised him reincarnation as a rock-and-roll
god if only he'd come over to the other side. Before long, he
was spending most of his time in Norwich State Hospital,
where the psychotropic drugs of the era quickly turned a
beautiful young man greasy, fat, and pockmarked. Out
again, he took acid and fell apart completely, walking into
the woods and never showing up for dinner. Another
friend, Larry Groff, and I found him two days later, lying on
a rock, his pants full, staring up blankly at the trees, bab-
bling reiteratively:

> *"Be my friend and I'll turn you on!*
> *Be my friend and I'll turn you in!"*

Later on, as K.B. was being checked back into Norwich
one more time, he excused himself from the admissions office to go to the bathroom. He was found hanging there a
few minutes later; the hospital hadn't yet confiscated his
belt.

Most of my friends were smoking pot and dropping acid
before they'd ever tasted beer or wine. Indeed, we were
downright snooty about alcohol—it was a drug for our
parents or for the lunkheaded, fat-bellied "beer freaks" who
lived down near Willimantic and delighted in torturing
longhairs. For all our talk of universal brotherhood—and
some of us really did talk that way—a majority of the entitled faculty kids, myself definitely included, were deeply
snobbish toward working-class Storrs.

Yet it was the Workers' Revolution that introduced us

to booze. Larry, the sole remotely convincing Marxist-Leninist in our grade, and a person of great warmth and humor, despite his temporary incarnation as a sixteen-year-old Robespierre, had switched over to the Progressive Labor Party after the Students for a Democratic Society split apart in 1969. The PLP originated as a quasi-Maoist organization but would break with China's "Great Helmsman" and denounce him as a revisionist after he met with Nixon in 1972. (Mao must have been crushed.) I never thought much of the Party but PLP did throw great *parties,* usually fund-raisers for the latest twenty-year-old suburban Comrade locked up in the fetid Seyms Street jail in Hartford. At these events, illegal drugs were banned as "counterrevolutionary," but beer and wine flowed freely and a whole crowd of involuted, inhibited, navel-gazing teenage freaks discovered the liberating effects of alcohol.

I liked it from the start—the tingling sense of permission it gave, the enhanced conviviality, the diminution of self-consciousness, and the temporary immunity from personal demons that it provided—and I continue to like it today. The world is disentangled; things make sense. As the novelist Dawn Powell (of whom I'd not yet heard) put it in one of her novels about Manhattan, *The Happy Island*:

> Yes, he was tight now and he thought what a
> splendid word it was. "Tight"—the moment
> when your words and deeds swell up to fit your
> sagging personality, leaving not a chink for
> reason to probe, not a crease where dignity can
> hide; now you are tight, neat, exactly as big as

> you are small and small as you are big; now the
> lens of the mind magnifies to include only the
> immediate object, this match flame, this
> forefinger.

I've been an enthusiastic drinker ever since, although most of my European friends put me to shame and I far prefer the physical act of drinking to the condition of being drunk. I've cut back dramatically on several occasions and quit once altogether, during which time I suffered no withdrawal symptoms but felt a huge surge in my social awkwardness that grew worse with each passing month. When I wasn't at work, I sat in my apartment, rocking back and forth, playing the same music over and over while watching the Weather Channel on cable television with the sound turned off. I had by then been diagnosed with Asperger's syndrome and, once I returned to wine again, it felt as though I had reintroduced a central solvent that my body chemistry had been missing for the better part of a year. I am not inclined to repeat the experiment.

SEVEN

Outside the Campus Restaurant. Storrs, 1972.

For a long time, I considered my life story one of a charmed kid who had been able to write novels, play the piano, compose, make movies, and even earn a little fame before he reached his teens but then threw it all into a dung heap, started smoking, drinking, and taking drugs, and basically wrecked his future. My father certainly believed this to be the case at the time, and it is true that there was little tangible evidence of growth over the next few years. I quit piano lessons; my few films were unwatchable stoned-out streams of semi-consciousness that panned to the sun every fifteen seconds; and my written output consisted of either graveyard poetry or first drafts of horrid, pretentious stories with characters named Rex Valve and Rosetta Stone.

In retrospect, I take a more charitable view of those years. For all the mistakes I made in my late teens—and they were considerable—I now believe that they were also inevitable, if I was to take any baby steps toward authenticity. Slowly, I became less walled within myself, more willing to give and take, more cognizant of human values. If I was still stuck in parallel play, at least I was sitting closer to my playmates.

From 1970 to 1975—the three years during which I was ostensibly finishing Edwin O. Smith High School and then for another two thereafter—I spent most of my days in the Campus Restaurant, which stood directly across the street from the school, a perfect place to cut a class or, for that matter, a whole day of them. It was run by a pair of brothers, Henry and Ed Wong, and had occupied most of a large, windowless basement in the center of Storrs since 1956. You could show up at eight in the morning, buy a cup of coffee, and then read, talk, or play chess until the restaurant closed at 8:45 PM. People *lived* there.

The Campus Restaurant was the epicenter of Storrs Hip, an outpost of Cambridge and Berkeley. It was the place where visiting counterculture dignitaries, from Jean Genet to Leonard Cohen, were brought when they came through town, where demonstrations were plotted, where lecherous old professors came to grope stoned college girls through their filmy blouses. In addition to the top hits, the jukebox had singles by Nat Adderley, Miles Davis, Nina Simone, as well as Jefferson Airplane, Country Joe and the Fish, and several short-lived local bands. The bulletin board was a forum for extracurricular activities, keeping everybody informed of the latest astral doings of Sri Chinmoy, Guru Maharaji, Elizabeth Clare Prophet, and the perfect masters of Eckankar, as well as fifty-seven varieties of leftism. Anyone in search of a support group for physically challenged Third World vegetarian internationalist Lesbians for Christ in Storrs would do well to start the quest at the Campus Restaurant.

Each September, neatly groomed new UConn faculty members and their families would descend the front stairs and pay what usually wound up as their one and only visit to the spot. On the landing, through a haze of cigarette smoke, they would survey the scene—gloomy longhairs with walrus mustaches and bleary eyes staring up from Penguin Modern Classics, teens shaking the pinball machines until they tilted, unleashed dogs wandering from table to table in clear defiance of Connecticut health department regulations, sometimes urinating on poles or legs—and then quickly pivot around and walk up and out.

Merely to be sighted entering the Campus Restaurant enhanced one's local notoriety. The place was thoroughly clique-ridden, with an internal pecking order that might have flummoxed the most seasoned New York maître'd. Longtime patrons had their own section; it was unmarked, but everybody knew where it was and to sit there without proper invitation qualified as a shocking faux pas. The brothers kept a snarling German shepherd, named Fritz, behind the counter and, every now and then, Eddy Wong would take a violent dislike to a customer and throw him out bodily. There was no table service; you placed your order at the counter and one of the Wongs would call out when your food was ready, either by the dish you had ordered ("Grilled cheese on rye!") or, if you had really arrived, by your name. An élite few even had house accounts.

One year, part of the exterior sign broke off, and drivers-by on Route 195 must have been startled that anybody would think to open an establishment with the unappetizing name PUS RESTAURANT. But the Wongs seemed in no hurry to fix the matter, and it entertained the regulars, who began calling the place "the Pus." Few customers would have made extravagant claims for the food, anyway—one friend went so far as to bring his own lunch from home every day to eat it, unmolested, at a central table—and the coffee was variously likened to grease or motor oil.

When the Campus finally closed in the autumn of 1977, to be replaced by a hamburger chain, which traded in its graffiti-canaled wooden tables for bright red Formica, even the lofty *Hartford Courant* took notice. Terese Karmel's article ran under the headline "Closing of Restaurant Ends Way of Life": she described the Campus as "a meeting place, message center, lending library, café, music-and-game room and classroom." Diana Lee, identified as a UConn drama student, volunteered that it was "the only place where freaks could go and feel welcome."

All in all, it was the strangest establishment I ever knew, and the one to which I would most like to return, with the stipulation that I could flee the moment I wanted to. Most of the customers thrived on their misery—"I can remember awful raw November days when I was completely bummed out, and I spent most of the afternoon here with other bummed-out people," one patron told Karmel—and I was no exception as I sat there for hours, watching the Campus fill up and empty, playing Tom Rush's recording of "Urge for Going" again and again on the jukebox. The Campus was a place to kill time, strike poses, to wallow in confusion while, as the poet John Berryman put it, "waiting for fame to descend with a scarlet mantle and tell us who we were."

A couple of decades on, there would be a great deal of fuss made over so-called "political correctness." I grew suspicious of the term, for it seemed to imply that simple human respect for people with different backgrounds was somehow a trendy and repressive fad. And yet I confess that I grew terribly tired of the reflexive radicalism I found in the counterculture.

By the early 1970s, the Friday Film Series, that longtime sanctuary for Storrs intellectuals, where I had received my indoctrination into Bergman and Truffaut, was suddenly filled with stoned brats who snickered through love scenes (even those in *Sunrise*), mocked any character in a uniform, and called out snide would-be witticisms throughout the program. It was horrible, and I stopped attending if anything more serious than *Duck Soup* was being shown. Moreover, I had become pals with one of the UConn police officers, a sweet, wryly funny black man named Chip Jenkins. He could belt out soul ballads with the best of them (we would sometimes improvise blues songs together), and it enraged me to hear him described as a "pig."

Then again, I was once called a pig myself. Kevin Cawley

and I were on our way to get cigarettes at the local A & P when we were accosted by one of the most aggressive leftists we knew, stationed outside with a battle-hardened grimace and a pile of leaflets.

"You're not going to buy any lettuce, are you?" he asked.

We weren't, and told him so—why, did we look like people who were going to buy lettuce?

"Because if you're going to buy lettuce you're both pigs," he rattled on, as though he hadn't heard us. And he broke into a lecture about the United Farm Workers lettuce boycott—which, in retrospect, stands out as a substantial and heroic accomplishment. Unfortunately, his speech was delivered through a prism of Revolutionary Youth Movement rhetoric, much of it quite insulting.

We promptly went into the store, bought our cigarettes, and added a head of iceberg to the order, after which we kicked it around like a soccer ball in the parking lot until it fell apart, as our interlocutor cursed us with all the Marxian invective he had at his disposal.

Fundamentalism of any stripe—religious, aesthetic, or political—had always been abhorrent to me, and there came a time when left-wing politics began to enter a Puritan orbit. At an outdoor party, I succumbed to the silent entreaties of a friendly, lop-eared puppy and broke off a piece of my hamburger.

"Oh, no!" a young woman shouted across the yard. "You gave him *meat*?"

I admitted as much.

"How could you? He's a *vegetarian*!"

I hadn't realized that there was such a thing—nor, I suspect, had the dog, who was now licking his chops and watching me intently, tail wagging like a windshield wiper.

At least the owner of the world's first vegetarian dog was an optimist. The Campus Restaurant was increasingly filled with glum, pseudosocialist realist posters of stone-faced, rainbow-hued members of what we called the Oppressed Nation of the Week Club, in what seemed a just struggle to unclench their fists.

Kevin and I devised a way to mock the movement hard-liners, who so prided themselves on being on top of every cause and secret. ("Like, it wouldn't be cool for me to tell you where the Weathermen are hiding, but I can promise you this—we're just like brothers.") When we had some-how been stuck with one of these bores, who brandished their Lenin the way an evangelist brandishes a Bible, we would break into a private game. It went like this: We'd start talking, with confidence and heat, about a purportedly state-sanctioned slaughter of a tribe of escaped laboratory monkeys that had taken place in the mythical town of Dunesville, Ohio. We argued opposing sides, creating de-tails as the story proceeded, setting a trap for whoever might be listening to us.

"Look, man, the police *had* to act," I might say, taking the conservative line. "After the multinational team of veteri-narians said they could do nothing about it, and the mon-keys were leaping on cars and tearing up cornfields and there were all those accidents all over the Ohio Turnpike, what would *you* have done?"

"It was slaughter, pure and simple, just like Kent *State*, man," Kevin would counter. "Those cops didn't have to fire—after all, we're only a few genes away from wild monkeys ourselves."

"*Bull*shit, man . . ." And on we went. Sometimes our intended prey would admit that he knew nothing of the incident, in which case we might crack up, confess that it was all a put-on, and occasionally make a new friend. We were far happier when the person treated us to a lengthy class analysis of the "on-the-scene situation in Dunesville," and our greatest triumph came when one SDS type pulled up his shirt, pointed to what was obviously an appendix scar, and announced soberly that it was a wound he had received during a righteously violent confrontation to "save the Dunesville monkeys, man." His stature never recovered.

Like Kevin, my friend Dean Cook was astonishingly quick and funny. I was at his house once when he received an unsolicited call from the local bowling alley, informing him that he had won a chance for a free week of lessons. "Is this some kind of sick joke?" he screamed into the phone. "I don't have any arms or legs!"

Dean grew up only a few houses down the street, so I spent a great deal of time with him from early childhood onward. It began as a friendship of convenience—it's a lot easier to play with a kid from the neighborhood than with one who lives five miles away—but it turned into one of the closest associations of my life. In our teen years, we'd sneak a couple of beers, smoke our cigarettes, and make vicious adolescent fun of television shows:

Here's the story
Of a lovely lady
Who was bringing up three very lovely girls.
All of them had hair of gold
Like their mother
The youngest one had balls.

Much of our friendship was based on mutual mockery; any weak spots either of us had were an invitation to poke and tease. In life, you'll find very few people with whom you share a unique laughter that belongs only to the two of you, and it is one of the highest forms of communication.

The sole recurring dream of my adulthood involves Dean. He was killed in my senior year of college when a group of drunks coming from a Willimantic bar crashed into the car in which he was a passenger just as it was turning left on a blind curve. Dean was obliterated instantly—it was estimated that the other car was going almost a hundred miles an hour—and his driver woke up a month or two later with no memory of what had happened.

Thereafter, a spectral Dean would visit me every few weeks. In the dream, he was always damaged—on crutches or horribly scarred or missing a limb. But I was invariably thrilled to see him, and I'd say something like "I'm sorry that you were hurt, but to tell you the truth this isn't so bad, because for a while there we were afraid that you were really going to die." At which point Dean would begin to fade away and I'd wake up, shaken with renewed grief.

I observe countless private anniversaries, and they affect

me like a fever. Right now I'm preparing for the thirtieth anniversary of Dean's death, and I wonder whether I'm the only person left who will spend most of that day in bed. Once somebody becomes a part of my life, I will let them out only for the most urgent of reasons. Death doesn't count. I'm not priding myself on my loyalty here: I'm loyal enough, but my brain isn't sufficiently agile to comprehend such seismic changes, and the world without my parents, without Dean, Kevin, Christopher, Leonard, and other people I've loved, is no more imaginable to me than the world without clouds, the color green, or the city of London. With no faith in ghosts or conviction in an afterlife, I nevertheless continue to honor my lost, my dead. I don't see that I have any choice in the matter, for they surround me and are with me always, regardless of their physical condition.

Most of my memories of these people involve music, our shared affinity for albums that we loved. I spent a summer infatuated with Frank Zappa, then suddenly found most of his work unpardonably snide. Still, my reading on Zappa led me to Captain Beefheart (born Don Vliet), whose music I took to right away, not only because I liked it but because it annoyed the hell out of others. Indeed, there was no faster way to clear out a Storrs party in the mid-1970s than to put on one of Beefheart's records and crank up the volume. It was like throwing a bomb. The rugged old Garrard turntable (widely favored in those days because it cost less than a hundred dollars at the college stereo shop) was traditionally stacked with chugalug paeans to Southern laxity from the Allman Brothers, excruciatingly sensitive analyses of love among the famous from Joni Mitchell and James

Taylor, endless jam sessions by the Grateful Dead, or—if the crowd happened to be unusually hip—explosive early disco from the Hues Corporation or Shirley & Company.

From the moment the phonograph needle settled into a Beefheart groove, however, everything changed. Aggressive crunching rent the air. Complicated time signatures and opaque poetry upset polite conversation and rattled the Mateus rosé. Beefheart's roar of purest gravel and the untrammeled violence of his rhythms sent timid souls into bummers; lovers could find no slow dances; young professors would sniff around the turntable, scrutinize the spinning disc, pronounce the music "um . . . *interesting*," and then move as far away from the loudspeakers as possible. Meanwhile, a small but significant counterforce of Beefheart fans would surround the captured stereo, beaming with anarchic triumph.

Another favorite band was Procol Harum, whose best songs combined haunted melodies, evocative words, sure formal construction, churchy consonance (in the passages for piano and organ), scathing dissonance (usually from the guitar), and the most purely musical drumming anywhere in rock. The group is remembered almost exclusively for its one big hit, "A Whiter Shade of Pale" and, over the years, I've been put out by a tendency among rock historians to place the band with Yes, Emerson, Lake & Palmer, Weather Report, and the remainder of the "Hey-lookit-me-I'm-playing-in-$\frac{7}{4}$!" pseudo-virtuosi of the early 1970s. But I was already temperamentally uncomfortable with display for its own sake, and what attracted me to Procol Harum's best tracks was the sense that every note was there for a musical reason, without which the overall structure would be diminished.

I had never worried about responding to unpopular music—indeed, I thrived on it—but I remember feeling more than a little embarrassment when I realized that I was becoming a passionate admirer of the later Beach Boys records. No group had ever fallen so far so fast in public esteem: they had devolved from the most popular American band of the early 1960s to a doddering relic of all that we were supposed to want to leave behind us in our brave new Utopia.

Brian Wilson had turned inward. Instead of churning out more of the luminous, catchy three-minute paeans to surfing, cars, girls, and the "California dream" that had made his fortune, he withdrew from the commercial world and began to produce vaporous, ethereal, elaborately ornamented musical clockworks, distinguished by a blossoming tenderness and sheer sonic splendor. This is no longer any secret, of course: Wilson is now both a mainstream American cultural hero *and* an abiding saint to the perennial pop-music avant-garde, a difficult combination that no one else could have pulled off. Still, the fact remains that the Beach Boys, with their legacy of hot rods, striped shirts, and middle-class Pacific values, were a tough sell to jaded, would-be-revolutionary Connecticut teens in the 1970s, and I kept my admiration mostly to myself.

And then there was *Forever Changes*, by Arthur Lee and his band Love. Never a hit—dozens of records in 1967 out-sold *Forever Changes* many times over—it never quite went out of print, either, and, year after year, devotees passed copies on to new listeners (I caught up with it around 1972), with the result that its legion of fans is unusually multigenerational. Imagine taking one of the most tuneful and adventurous pop albums by the Byrds and allowing it to marinate for a year or two in the most decadent and exotic spices. Then stir in some of the unhinged paranoia of Syd Barrett and the early Pink Floyd, the reclusive melancholy of post-surf Brian Wilson, the cotton-candy orchestration of sixties arrangers like Paul Mauriat or Joshua Rifkin and set it to dark and prophetic lyrics that seem to mean much more than they dare to say, and presto!—*Forever Changes*. The album combined a seductive surface prettiness with a sense of imminent danger—psychedelia at its edgiest.

Outside of Arthur Lee, I knew very little black music then—a few favorite Fats Waller recordings, some Count Basie and Louis Armstrong, a smidgen of Miles Davis, the raunchier songs of Bessie Smith, the startling debut by the prodigious Shuggie Otis. I would be in my late twenties before I learned anything about soul and rhythm and blues—the genres just weren't a part of the almost all-white youth culture of eastern Connecticut—although I would respond immediately to the washed-out, don't-wake-me desolation of Sly & the Family Stone's *There's a Riot Goin' On*, which was somehow classified as rock. A very different response to pain infuses John Lennon's first solo disc, a powerful succession of intensely personal songs, many of them punctuated by wrenching shrieks, created when he was undergoing a radical form of psychotherapy with Arthur Janov.

I went so far as to buy Janov's book *The Primal Scream*,

which impressed me mightily and inspired several amateur attempts to elicit such cleansing howls myself. But most of my reading was in the underground press (*Rolling Stone, Rock,* and *Crawdaddy!*), and I dreamed of writing about classical music with the energy and freedom I so admired in pop reviews. An innate formal prissiness probably kept me from responding to the Beat writers. I liked their message, but not what seemed to me a lot of arbitrary, loquacious, and unmusical choices of words. Nobody could accuse Vladimir Nabokov of careless writing, but a lifelong detestation of puzzles and word games mostly put me off him until years later, when I encountered *Speak, Memory.* And I had a natural allergy to Carlos Castaneda, J. R. R. Tolkien, Mervyn Peake, C. S. Lewis, and the rest of the fantasists who were then so popular. Their books struck me as kid stories for grown-ups, and I hadn't liked kid stories even when they were age-appropriate.

The writings that spoke most urgently to me in my late teens were the novels of the French existentialists, especially Sartre's *Nausea* and Camus's *The Fall,* which served both to ground my pessimism and to bolster my resolve to continue anyway. ("There is only one true philosophical question and that is Suicide"—Jim Morrison spent his whole career trying to match that line!) And then, attracted by the detail from a Diego Rivera mural on its cover, which called to mind my father's old volume of *Modern Mexican Art,* I bought *Under the Volcano.* It was tough going at first, and I made a couple of false starts before buckling down one night and reading through all of its 350-odd pages in what I remember as a marathon sitting. Stunned by the novel's evocation of chaos and fear, its stark Sophoclean majesty, I carried it everywhere, reading it again and again, one paperback edition eroding into the next. Years later, during my first adult visit to the United Kingdom, there were two places to which I made pilgrimages: Gough Court in London, where Samuel Johnson assembled the first dictionary of the English language, and the village of Ripe, where I ceremoniously poured a beer over the grave of Malcolm Lowry.

EIGHT

Playing electric piano with headphones in the early
morning of May 20, 1972, in Storrs.

My depression arrived like a Midwestern summer thunderstorm—clouds moving in slowly, balletically, in strange air and mustard light. Everything I read, watched, and listened to was unrelievedly gloomy, and this was having its effect. By the time I was seventeen, I had begun to think regularly of killing myself and even went so far as to type out a self-conscious suicide note one night, leaving it on my desk, doubtless to be found by my poor mother:

> Dear Mom, Dad, Rick, Betsy, Gaga and Kerry*—
> To use an old line, by the time you get this, I

*Kerry was the family poodle.

will be dead. If this is a coward's way out I am
sorry. This life just doesn't have it for me
anymore. My mind is shot. All there is in this
world is pain and insanity. Do not pity me.
I will finally find peace and quiet.

I divvied up my possessions, noting that any records my
brother and sister didn't want were to go to Dean. I ap-
pended a short list of people I wanted informed of my love
for them, and added, "Tell the others to go to hell." There
were some passive-aggressive jabs at my father: "I'm sorry
for ruining *your* life so badly." I requested burial with my
toy dog Mario and to have a Procol Harum song played at
my funeral. To make the note as dramatic as I could, I
signed it "Tim Page (1954–1971)."

Selfish, juvenile posturing, to be sure—I doubt that I'd
even begun to explore a method of self-extinction—but the
letter was impelled by genuine misery, which only increased with the panic attacks that had suddenly begun to
affect me.

Like everything else back then, these started at the Campus Restaurant. In addition to what had become a leaden,
chronic unhappiness, there were at least three outside trig-
gers for my first bout of hyperventilation: the coffee I was
drinking all day; the cigarettes I was chain-smoking (non-
filtered Camels or English Ovals); and the marijuana that I
was still forcing upon myself, as an attempt to maintain ritual communion with my friends, even after it had become
abundantly apparent that the drug was no longer for me.

Suddenly, while playing a game of pinball one winter

day, I couldn't get my breath. It felt as though I were inhaling liquid, perhaps my own blood, and I gulped as much oxygen as I could force into what seemed to be my drowning lungs. My hands and feet went numb, my chest constricted, I couldn't speak, and I was convinced that my heart was stopping. The Campus Restaurant took on an Orange Sunshine unreality, and I ran outdoors and rolled around and around in the snow until I was too cold to think and psychological pains ceded mercifully to physical ones.

My second such spell took place in the middle of a dental appointment, set off by the numbness I felt from the Novocain, which spread down from my puffy face throughout my entire body, a cessation of feeling that I was certain would prove lethal. Dr. Silverman halted the drilling several times, as I twitched and panted and rearranged myself in the chair, squirming under the hot bright lights. I was determined to be brave but I just couldn't manage, and after a while I was convulsing and crying and screaming "I'm dying!" over and over at the top of my lungs. (I can only imagine what other patients, riffling nervously through last week's *Time* magazine in the waiting room, must have thought.) An M.D. in the building rushed upstairs to examine me. He reassured me that my vital signs were normal and that this was most likely an anxiety attack; my problem was not that I was getting too little oxygen but that I seemed to be getting too much. He found a brown paper bag and put it over my nose and mouth to control the over-breathing and to allow some carbon dioxide back into my system. He also gave me a Valium, which was dispensed as readily as aspirin then. (In a 1979 movie called *Starting Over*, Burt Reynolds collapses into a panic attack at Bloomingdale's, a very good place for one. "Does anybody have a Valium?" he gasps, and the spectators who have gathered reach unanimously into pockets and purses.)

The words of FDR's first inaugural speech—"The only thing we have to fear is fear itself"—now took on literal meaning for me, as I was perpetually frightened and ever fearful of growing more so. I drastically curtailed my activities; I sat with my back to the wall in the Campus Restaurant and on the aisle in the College Theater. If I went into any city, even Willimantic, I would need to be fortified by tranquilizers or a few drinks. When I made it to school at all, I'd sit by the door and slip out when I felt the numbness start to kick in, as it invariably would once I thought of it.

Annie's mother taught at E.O. Smith High School and was always loving and supportive, no matter what I was up to. Most of the music teachers were less pleased, as I regularly corrected their factual errors while still managing to flunk their general exams. But I did find one mentor in the English department, an elderly woman named Laura Singer, who taught the school's most advanced writing class. She was formal and famously strict—she still gave out F's, which were already beginning to disappear (although I had managed to collect a few of them). My guidance counselor did her best to dissuade me from taking Mrs. Singer's course, and everybody predicted disaster—the faux "free spirit" versus the supposedly fussy schoolmarm.

It so happened that we loved each other from the start.

Mrs. Singer had lived in Greenwich Village when she was young, and her husband ran the bookstore above the Campus Restaurant. We shared a keen interest in modern literature, and she had met some of its distinguished practitioners. She was the first person outside my family who actually believed that I could write; she recognized my anxiety and accepted it, permitting me to cut her classes when necessary, with the agreement that if I would continue to turn in assignments she would continue to let me pass. And she was better than her word; she gave me the only A's I ever received in high school, the first of which astonished me so much that I thought there must be some mistake.

My father had been a talented, lyrical writer himself, but his standards were impossibly high and after two or three rejection slips from *The New Yorker* for unheralded story submissions, he gave up fiction altogether. He read my work for Mrs. Singer and encouraged me warmly, and it marked the first close communication we'd had in several years. He was also delighted to hear me practice Beethoven's *Sonata Quasi una Fantasia* (Op. 27, No. 1), universally known as the "Moonlight" sonata. He had never taken lessons but, by force of will, had taught himself to play the famous first movement by heart and with no little sensitivity.

After Caracas I no longer had a piano teacher, but I played for several hours every day and became pretty good; the first sonata by the Argentine composer Alberto Ginastera was a favorite, for it looks and sounds much harder than it is and is so dissonant that only a trained listener is able to discern any mistakes. Still, I approached the instrument as a composer, not as a pianist, and I had little regard for the technical finish that would have required concentrated work on scales and arpeggios, which I found too boring to contemplate. The music that interested me was played with authority and some originality, but I fudged my way through a lot of it.

One summer my mother, always in hope of a miracle, determined that I should go away to what is now the Tanglewood Music Center in Lenox, Massachusetts. The soft beauty of the ancient hills, the intimate contact with artists from around the world, the consecrated professionalism that pervaded my experience there—it was nothing short of an awakening. Suddenly I had peers who understood (and sometimes shared) my obsessions, with whom I could discuss the pieces I was learning on the piano, the compositions I was trying to write, obscure recordings, the proper way to dot a sixteenth note, and the dream of what Glenn Gould called the purpose of art—"a gradual, lifelong construction of a state of wonder and serenity."

Lenox was full of giants in those days. There was sweet-tempered, loosely knit Aaron Copland in the Tanglewood library, elucidating his magnificent *Piano Variations* to adoring acolytes. Leonard Bernstein, tanned and vigorous in an open-necked pink shirt, not yet the grand old man he later became but already legendary, would walk through the main gate and our cafeteria talk would come to a temporary halt. When he waved in our general direction, such was the Bernstein charisma that everyone at our table felt specifically singled out by his greeting.

Mondays through Thursdays, students and musicians

had Tanglewood pretty much to themselves. Not so on the weekends, when concert-hungry trekkers from New York, Boston, and every place in between would descend on us. By late morning on Fridays, the "No Vacancy" signs were on and blinking most of the way down Route 7 to the Connecticut border. Lenox, the center of summer activity in the Berkshires, would be congested with automobiles and, despite the best efforts of the traffic cops, there were the usual near-collisions at the irregular intersection where Walker Street meets the Lenox-Pittsfield Road. The better restaurants would be booked through Sunday, and merchants extended their hours with the hope that the brief, bustling season might pay the bills through the cloistered winter just ahead.

During Boston Symphony Orchestra concerts, the Tanglewood lawn was divided into distinct audiences. Serious listeners sat near the entrance to the Shed, with scores, books, or Sunday newspapers spread open on their blankets. Picnickers were everywhere; silence ruled within some fifty yards of the orchestra, while wine and conversation flowed freely farther on. Way over by the Main House, children laughed, played, and turned cartwheels, bothering nobody, oblivious to the Beethoven but alert to the joys of a clement summer afternoon.

It was at Tanglewood that I first came to know a good number of gay people and for once in my life I encountered a new (to me) human variant without any sort of initial prejudice or discomfort. If anything, having always found sex mysterious and complicated for my own reasons, it was reassuring to find some company outside the supposed mainstream. I certainly never felt any threat to my own identity, which was always heterosexual, however squeamishly. The two or three homosexual dreams I've had over the years lacked eroticism and I never counted them as anything beyond interesting curiosities, deserving of no more serious analysis than last night's dream of befriending a talking llama.

I got on less well with some of the zealous young composers I met at Tanglewood. The personal politics of the great modernist composers tended to be moderate or even conservative; still, it has always seemed to me that a parallel might be drawn between modernism and Marxism, both of whose followers used to envision history as an irresistible and logical flow. Modernists clung to the same breathless belief in "progress"—Bach led inevitably to Mozart, to Beethoven, to Wagner, and on to Schoenberg and . . . well, to *them*. In the long heyday of chromatic modernism, I heard it argued that although most of the public had systematically rejected atonal music for the better part of a century, eventually listeners would catch up to it, and all budding composers had a duty to proceed accordingly, with unshakable faith in that most unreliable of chimeras, the future. I loved a lot of this music—Anton Webern, Ralph Shapey, Karlheinz Stockhausen, and Milton Babbitt were four of my favorite composers—but I saw no reason that its propagation should be any sort of one true faith.

A strict barrier between so-called "popular" and "serious" music still prevailed, except among the younger Tanglewood students. I felt no need to limit my own listening, and passed a good deal of my time suited up in headphones at the Lenox Library, where a couple of tracks from a new pop record might follow a side of *Der Rosenkavalier.* Years later, a reader would take me to task for an article I wrote expressing admiration for the very different talents of Webern and Van Morrison in the same paragraph, with no attempt to establish a ranking order. But such blanket hierarchies always seemed silly to me—about as profound and meaningful as saying "New Zealand is better than Germany"—and my listening tastes grew ever more eclectic at Tanglewood.

Part of this derived from a new immersion in the history of twentieth-century music, a subject long taught as some sort of gladiatorial death bout between the followers of Arnold Schoenberg and Igor Stravinsky. Suddenly neither of these figures seemed so totemic, and the works of other important creators were factored into my understanding— the stark, runic middle period of Sibelius, the musical cubism of Leos Janáček, the radiant late flowering from Richard Strauss, and the confessional string quartets of Shostakovich, for example. Meanwhile, I was listening to proudly regional work, from Eastern Europe, Scandinavia, Africa, and Asia—as well as to rock and jazz.

For all this merging and melding, I never thought much of so-called crossover music. It always seemed to me that jazz needed classical music about as much as a discotheque needs whaling songs. And the very specificity of rock records—the fused, symbiotic relationship between artist and song—made it difficult to incorporate this music within the boundaries of a classical concert. Traditional pop standards such as "Misty," "Stormy Weather," and "As Time Goes By" were designed to be played in a wide variety of different arrangements, by wildly divergent artists. But when I wanted to hear "She's a Rainbow," I wanted to hear it from the Rolling Stones, not from the Boston Pops or, indeed, from anybody else. Recordings were becoming an art form in themselves, increasingly separated from live experience.

(Years later, late at night in all-but-deserted bars near Tanglewood or Carnegie Hall, where critics would gather to drink, dish, and argue the merits and demerits of concerts recently attended, some friends and I used to play an invented parlor game called the Worst Records Never Made. The point was to hypothesize the most stunningly inappropriate albums we could imagine—pairings of artists and material so horrific that even the famously dunderheaded major labels would hardly consider making them. Most of our inspirations have been lost to memory, but the notion of discs like "Yodel with the Berlin Philharmonic," "The Three Tenors Sing Gilbert and Sullivan," and—my favorite—"The Chipmunks Present Your Favorite Spirituals" can still inspire what P. G. Wodehouse used to call "the raised eyebrow, the sharp intake of breath.")

That summer, I loved all that was anguished and apocalyptic in music, and swore by the lapel-shaking excesses of the gloomiest Mahler—the Sixth and Ninth symphonies and the torso of the unfinished Tenth. If certain songs from certain bands can be described as "feel-good music," this is feel-*bad* music—haunted studies in introversion that exact a passionate subjective reaction from sympathetic admirers, depressed adolescents naturally among them. I mistrusted anything that was less than capital-C Cosmic—the sky opening up, the Truth revealed—and I would probably have agreed with the pianist Claudio Arrau, who famously insisted that there was no humor in Beethoven's music.

Today, I would be more likely to argue that there was no humor in Claudio Arrau, for a great deal of Beethoven, and much of what I value most, is cheerily good-natured and sometimes even hilarious. And I'm convinced that it is our long-standing cultural tendency to equate seriousness with profundity that has kept us from taking the full measure of Gioacchino Rossini. For me, he is among the greatest of musical geniuses. No other creator could have concocted the first-act finale of the opera *L'Italiana in Algeri,* for example, when the action spins magnificently out of control and language is no longer sufficient to express the loopy feelings of the characters, who are reduced to rapid-fire onomatopoeia—"ding! ding!" and "cra! cra!" and "tac! tac!," and that perennial favorite "boom boom boom boom boom boom *boom!*"

If Chico Marx had written an opera libretto, it might have sounded something like this. It is Dada a hundred years before Dada was invented. But it is better than Dada, for it is less a mockery of convention than the construction of a gleeful parallel universe, one stocked with indelible tunes. And then there is the celebrated Rossini crescendo— a melodic fragment repeated three times over, with increased volume and intensity as it grows, a gesture both utterly predictable and ever new, into which the listener sinks as if it were a bath.

But it was Hector Berlioz who struck me as the most misunderstood of composers. To this day, Berlioz is best known for one of his least representative pieces, the early *Symphonie Fantastique,* which typecast him as a disheveled, opium-munching romantic who channeled his hallucinations into music. And yet the composer's operatic masterpiece, *Les Troyens,* which I discovered in the Tanglewood music library, presents a very different sensibility. This five-act, four-hour pageant of dance and music drama is shot through with a chaste, high-minded nobility unlike anything else in the repertory. It is a radical work in many ways—certainly some of the harmonies in *Les Troyens* would not become commonplace for the better part of a century after it was written—but it looks gloriously backward for impetus, to the writings of Homer and Virgil, the stoicism of Greece and Rome, the timeless values of the Classical.

Les Troyens immediately became one of my favorite operas, yet it would be another thirteen years before I actually attended a performance—circumstances that would have startled Berlioz. To this day, in my mind Jon Vickers and Josephine Veasey are always singing the leading roles, as they did on the first complete recording of the work (the *only* recording for a quarter of a century), which I must have played a thousand times, to the point that I knew the performance as well as I knew the music being performed. (And how *do* you tell the dancer from the dance?) An older generation, weaned on the recordings of its day, grew up expecting every horn player to make a mess of his part in

Beethoven's Ninth Symphony, as does the soloist in an early Felix Weingartner rendition from the 1930s, and, for many, Alfred Cortot's finger slips are an integral part of their early memories of Chopin's piano music. And so with me: when I think of the great love duet in *Les Troyens,* it may take me a moment to remember that it takes place in Act Four, but I can remember precisely where to put down the tone arm on side 8 of the Philips five-record set to find the voices of Vickers and Veasey eternally intertwined.

Back in Storrs, filled with new philosophies and enthusiasms, I teamed up with a guitarist, a bassist, and two drummers to form a band. We called ourselves Dover Beach, after the poem by Matthew Arnold, and affected a romantic despair appropriate to our model. I wore a funeral cape onstage and wrote a forty-five-minute rock symphony called "Prometheus Unbound," which featured fragments of the Latin mass and strange chords that were sustained for minutes at a time. We were distinctly unpopular at frat parties.

I can't tell if our music was necessarily very good, but it was definitely unusual, especially considering that it was written and played by high-school kids. We were in fact experimenting with a rudimental form of what would later be called minimalism, and I've sometimes wondered what would have happened if somebody in the music business had heard us, cleaned us up, and brought us to New York. Instead, we performed at homes for delinquent girls, at the Mansfield Training School, and in soggy dives around eastern Connecticut. Our longest engagement was a three-night gig at the Dean's Office, one of the rowdiest bars in

Willimantic, and after the first show—when it had become obvious that "Prometheus Unbound" might just get us murdered—we spent the next day cramming to learn a lot of danceable tunes by the Doors and Savoy Brown.

Up to that point, the only cover version we'd done was of the Velvet Underground's "What Goes On," which we would stretch out for ten minutes or more, just the way the Velvets had themselves, as we would discover when the posthumous *Live in 1969* album was released a few years later. It is a song that should always seem as though it will go on playing forever; the melody and lyrics aren't very special, but oh, those rattling, eternal chords, pouring down like manna!

Chords and textures interested me more than the solos that rode over them. As such, I habitually listened more closely to the background of modern jazz recordings than to the foreground. And one of the things I loved about early minimalism was how very little sense of narrative it had. Unlike a traditional Western piece that might start softly, build to a crescendo, and then finish with some kind of proclamation or just fade away, a good minimalist piece simply *happened,* all at once, and then kept happening until it didn't. And so, as a listener, instead of wondering where the music might be going, you settled in and became stimulated by its *process* of going, as though you had boarded a train and thought nothing about where you'd been or where you were heading but merely surrendered yourself to jostle and speed and passing images.

Dover Beach was built on drones and chords and repetition. We broke up because nobody in Storrs liked us much, and we were getting to a point where we didn't much like one another. We had the ubiquitous band hassles, evoked so well in the film *This Is Spinal Tap*—egos, tensions between mates, endless rehearsals with little to show for them, no imaginable future. After we dissolved, all quarrels were put aside, and now when I meet up with members of Dover Beach we greet each other in much the same manner as veterans of long-ago pilgrimages, slightly amazed at all the things we did when we were young and crazy.

NINE

Jon H. Wetherell. Chaplin, Connecticut, Spring 1972.

Saturday nights were gatherings of the tribe. Somehow, either by hitchhiking or begging a ride from parents or older siblings, we would find our way to Rapp's Delicatessen, where the proprietor let us hang out and play pinball till closing. Nothing in the world mattered more to us than these weekly promenades. We could order a slice of pizza or a knish if we were hungry, and Rapp's had a good jukebox. More to the point, its parking lot was right next door to what the Connecticut blue laws still insist upon calling a "package store," outside which we would stand and implore hip-looking customers to take our underage change and fetch us back some Boone's Farm Apple Wine,

Old Mr. Boston Blackberry Brandy, or just a six-pack of Schlitz or Budweiser.

Once that was accomplished, we would break into groups, anteing up to purchase a dollar's worth of thirty-four-cents-a-gallon gas (thirty-one cents if you went to the Lehigh station, but the product was said to be inferior) and join whichever of our friends might have been entrusted with the family car that evening. Then we would drive around the back roads of Storrs, Ashford, and Coventry, consuming our beer and marijuana (the latter of which was much easier for teenagers to obtain) before the inevitable return to Rapp's. The police generally left us alone. We were mostly faculty kids, a status that gave us a certain cachet in what was then a class-riven town. (It would not do for a Willimantic cop to bust the daughter of a professor emeritus.) We'd listen to cassette tapes or to the new-fangled "eight-track" player, a brief-lived technological atrocity that would suddenly fade down the music in the middle of a song, make a curious *ka-CHUNK* sound, and then start up again.

On May 20, 1972, all of us had been drinking, as we did every Saturday night. But our livers were practically virgin then: it was quite possible for two people to share a quart of beer and end up giddy. So it was a catastrophic misfortune that our driver—an enormously likable young man of seventeen whom I will call Geoffrey, because that was not his name—had discovered Southern Comfort that evening, with no idea of its terrible potency. By the time we had jumped into his blue 1970 International pickup truck, impatient to experience speed and wind and what turned out to be a last few moments of teenage immortality on the cold spring night, Geoffrey was unsteady on his feet and in no condition to drive.

There was supposed to be a cast party up at the Mattingly house, to celebrate the opening of the E.O. Smith High School Drama Club production of *You Can't Take It with You.* The Drama Club was one of the few school-sponsored activities not entirely disdained by freaks. It was usually peopled with bright, fierce kids, more than a few of whom would eventually move in with partners of the same gender after they escaped what was then a pretty homophobic scene. (Gay rights were not high on the early counterculture agenda.) These students went to classes, earned good grades, and planned to attend college, yet they remained so urbane, ironic, and dismissive of such "uncool" activities that we had no problem accepting them as occasional companions.

Several of us decided to scout out the party. I hopped into the cab of Geoffrey's truck, squeezing in as close as I legitimately could to luscious Sandy, the girl seated in the middle. Three or four other people were sprawled in back (passengers in open trucks were common in those days, especially during the warm months, a bucolic vision now as far removed from American life as Huck and Jim on their raft). And then, as we waited for the traffic on Route 44 to release us from the parking lot, a group of much younger kids suddenly materialized and clambered aboard, so that we departed Rapp's with eleven riders.

This was insane, and Geoffrey knew it. But after he'd ordered the surplus passengers out of the truck, and after they'd all refused to budge, he took off in a rage, driving as rapidly and as roughly as possible, as though he intended to both thrill and punish everybody with an unrelentingly bouncy ride. Most of us were delighted, and we drove this way for about half a mile. Suddenly there was a pounding on the roof of the cab, and Geoffrey pulled over at the corner of Birch and Hunting Lodge. It was Kevin Martin and Mickey Chilleri, two of Geoffrey's closest friends and his partners in Southern Comfort earlier that evening. But Kevin, long fascinated with cars and motorcycles and already an expert driver, was angry. "What the hell is the matter with you?" he demanded. "Why don't you slow down? You're going to kill somebody!"

Further words were exchanged, and Kevin and Mickey jumped out of the truck to walk the rest of the way to the party. We took off again, and Geoffrey was even more agitated than before; he did not slow down, and the chaos intensified. Within a minute or two, we had arrived at the Mattingly's, but *You Can't Take It with You* was a longer play than anybody had anticipated and the house was still dark. So we opted to head back to Rapp's, roaring full speed down Hunting Lodge Road, and we had traveled just far enough for Kevin and Mickey to hear the shock, realize immediately what had happened, and come running up toward pandemonium.

. . . .

I was a passenger in my sister's vehicle, a 1968 Plymouth, traveling on Hunting Lodge Road in Mansfield. We were proceeding northbound when I observed a vehicle as we approached a curve in the road, heading toward us on what appeared to be two wheels. We began to slow down as this vehicle was beginning to swerve. At this time we came to a complete stop and watched the vehicle go by us. I believe it hit a telephone pole and then the vehicle began turning over. I believe it finally came to rest on its wheels. I got out of the car and proceeded toward the scene. As I approached I saw two individuals on the ground. One person was sitting with his back against a telephone pole. The other body was positioned on the side of the road. I tried to be of some assistance but my brother-in-law, who was at the scene, told us to leave. I called the University Infirmary to see if they had received any information as to the seriousness of the accident. I believe the Infirmary then called the State Police. I have read the above statement and it is the truth.

Sworn by Patricia S——, 5/21/1972, witnessed by State Trooper Clifford J. Lotz

. . . .

Vehicle rounded curve at high rate of speed, went off right side of road. Vehicle traveled 104 feet on dirt and grass shoulder prior to striking pole #CLP1420, then skidded back onto road. Impact of accident tore tailgate of right rear fender and body section from vehicle. Operator charged with misconduct with a motor vehicle.

He had an obvious odor of alcohol on his
breath. He appeared visibly nervous, and was
shaking and emotionally upset.

Connecticut Department of State Police Report,
5/21/1972, filed by State Trooper Clifford J. Lotz

• • • • • • • • • • • • • • • • • • •

Geoffrey had managed to avoid a head-on collision and
had instead slammed sideways into the pole, the impact
crushing the passenger door, collapsing the roof across the
cab, and tearing off much of the truck's right side. Had I
been restrained in place by a seatbelt, I would doubtless
have been killed. As it was, I lost consciousness for a few
minutes until I heard a girl's tearful voice pleading with me
through the darkness.

"Timmy, you've just *got* to get out of there!"

This suddenly seemed logical, and I awakened and
calmly extricated myself from the wreckage, as though
nothing had happened. At first glance, out on the street, the
scene didn't look so bad. Geoffrey and Sandy had both escaped injury, and most of the passengers in the truck bed
had flown into the night, only to pick themselves up where
they landed, unharmed.

Not all of them, though. The pole had sheared off eighteen-year-old Jon Wetherell, and thirteen-year-old Stephen
Hodovan, who had been sitting outdoors directly behind
me on the truck rim. Jon now lay motionless a few feet
away, his cheek on the sandy tar, one arm crooked behind
his back, as though he were preparing for a formal bow. I
knew that it was him, but I didn't know that it was him;

I regarded his presence with frigid composure, as though he were a bush or a piece of furniture, rather than one of my favorite people. (After all, this was vibrant, laughing, forever-cool Jon Wetherell—and he couldn't possibly be *dead*.) Stevie wandered around broken, coughing and heaving, his breath a spray of scarlet. "I'm going to die," he gasped to my friend Gary, who had known him since early childhood and who had arrived on the scene just before the police closed down the road. "You'll be all right, Stevie," Gary lied mercifully with as reassuring a smile as he could muster. And then there were sirens and red lights and stretchers, and we were taken to Windham Memorial Hospital in ambulances from four separate towns.

Michael Wilcox, the kindly minister at St. Mark's Episcopal Church, where I had once served as an altar boy, lived on Hunting Lodge Road and had walked to the scene. He phoned my family and told them that there had been an accident but that I seemed to be all right, adding that there were sure to be fatalities before the night was over. I was being examined near the entrance to the emergency room, and my parents, newly arrived, were watching me through little square windows in the double doors when I overheard Kevin formally identify the body of Jon Wetherell. As my face convulsed in grief, my father met my eyes and he raced in. Unwilling to believe what had happened, I asked him if it was true and he confirmed the news somberly, as an orderly begged him to leave the unprecedentedly busy ward. Stevie died a few minutes later—I knew it when Mr. Hodovan howled with fathomless horror and despair, a sound I will never forget—and I was shuttled past his clustered, sobbing sisters (he was the youngest of seven children and the only boy) to the room where I would spend the night under observation.

My left leg was broken and some rock-candy-size fragments of the windshield were embedded in my head, but I was otherwise unharmed. The doctor gave me some Valium to help me sleep, but I had grown accustomed to the drug by now and it didn't do much good. By the middle of the night, the hospital was quiet again, and I gazed up at the ceiling. I thought of a Pink Floyd song—one of the group's early, experimental suites—called "A Saucerful of Secrets," which opens with electronic sounds floating purposelessly through space, reaches a sudden, shattering climax, is followed by three or four minutes of percussive chaos, and eventually gives way to an ultra-calm Bachian chorale, complete with organ and chorus, suggesting a Hollywood vision of heavenly rest. To this day, I'm unable to hear "A Saucerful of Secrets" as anything other than a musical chronicle of May 20, 1972.

I was forbidden to attend the funerals, in part because I had a full cast on my leg and in part because poor Geoffrey had fallen apart so completely at the first one he attended that his mother called our house and urged my parents not to let me go. But I hobbled out to the graves a few days later, and I can still summon the confused, animal sense of loss I felt as I looked down at the rectangles of newly laid turf, which would green over slowly as the summer progressed. It was the very peak of a New England May—the air sweet with pollen, the dogwoods and magnolias already in flower, the tulips starting to bud—and the glorious weather only made what had happened more unreal. I tried to write about the accident, to find some sort of redemption in the horror, so that not everything would be lost, but I always gave up, for everything *was* lost this time. "We were young and none of us believed in death," one draft began, which was vaguely poetic, I suppose, but not really true. I had believed in death for a long time, but it had never come so close.

Storrs was different after that. It was a summer of sadness; it seemed that everybody knew somebody who had been in the truck (Wetherell, in particular, turned out to have had an amazing number of girls clandestinely in love with him), and every party ended in alcoholic weeping. It was a peculiar year, anyway; the woods were infested by an onslaught of gypsy moths, and by the beginning of August they had chewed the trees bare. There was some new, very strong marijuana around, but it was rumored to have been sprayed with Paraquat by the U.S. government in the hope of making smokers lose their minds. Both the Republicans and the Democrats held national conventions in Miami Beach, and the keener town politicos may have heard about a break-in at the Watergate office building in Washington, D.C.

We were growing up and scattering out—the end of childhood. A lot of the girls had first jobs, working as aides and orderlies at the Natchaug Nursing Home near Willimantic. My friend Liz returned from Europe with a newly elegant composure, and I was glad to hear tell of places where people were still waltzing. My friend Mark came back from a commune in Colorado, agleam with psychedelic radiance. It was thought that he had grown enlightened in his two months away, as he now grinned constantly, the most soft-eyed and benevolent of Buddhas, and some of us still half clung to the belief that wisdom could be swallowed in a pill, rather than slowly and imperfectly approached through time and suffering.

I have some marvelously immediate photographs of Wetherell, and only wish I could separate these joyful images from the fate that I now know awaited him, less than a month away. This is my eighteen-year-old friend who died, I can't help thinking—and that isn't fair to Jon, for he should not be defined by his abrupt departure from the world but by his abiding goodness during his life. I think I can still remember his voice, but I'm afraid that by now it's only the memory of the memory of that voice. But I do recall his lankiness, his easy grace, his ready sense of humor melded with an underlying seriousness, his slightly mismatched features all reconciled by a wide, radiant smile.

It was pure bad fortune that he had come to Storrs that night, for the Wetherells lived in another town, and Jon attended another high school. But he was nothing if not spontaneous. A few months earlier, after one of the local Kevins led us to believe that a factory town called Jewett City had loose and willing women in much the same profusion as Dick Whittington's mythical London had streets of gold, we had driven the better part of an hour to get there, only to find rows of drab clapboard houses and, after a search, a single drugstore with an open luncheonette.

"I heard Jewett City was a great place to pick up girls,"

Jon announced to the woman behind the counter, flashing his most debonair grin.

"Well, you heard wrong," she snapped, and stomped off to complain to the cook.

We hurried off to Tanglewood instead, where we lay around on the town green with a bunch of kids from Windsor Mountain School. "Lenox is a pretty hip scene," Jon said as we drove back well after midnight, and I was happy that he shared my enthusiasm, for that was a quality most of us had been trying stupidly to train out of ourselves. But Jon was all enthusiasm—for books, music, photography, and people. He loved a wine called Lake Niagara because, he claimed, it could taste like anything you wanted—and it *could,* but only in the company of Jon Wetherell. For years, Cory kept an empty bottle of Haffenreffer Private Stock malt liquor on his bureau. "That's from the last night I went juicing with Wetherell," he would explain to anybody who inquired, and the bottle instantly took on the stature of an iconic relic.

I visited Jon's grave on Tower Hill Road not long ago. It is an old grave now, an established part of an old cemetery. A quarter century ago, I might have sprinkled a little pot or poured a beer onto the ground as tribute. But Jon, too, would be in his fifties by now, and I cannot imagine that shared intoxications—once such a mysterious bond of brotherhood—would remain any more meaningful to him than they have for me. Nor do I believe that this gentle man would have wanted me to uproot living flowers to decorate his distant corner, which needed no such embellishment.

And so I simply sat in reflection, listening to the quiet, my head curiously empty, my senses overwhelmed.

Later that afternoon, I revisited the site of the accident and was startled by how maddeningly ordinary it was, the fatal curve nowhere near as fearsome as I remembered—nothing like the famous ones on Moulton Road or Dog Lane, for example. Hunting Lodge Road has now been developed to the extent that it is virtually a part of the University of Connecticut campus, and hundreds of people go by the spot every day, with no inkling of the tears shed for something that happened there so many years ago.

Nevertheless, May 20 is among the most somber of the anniversaries that I commemorate every year. I hope that Geoffrey has managed to forgive himself. He was a delightful guy, much loved, who happened to make a terrible, youthful mistake. It would be fatuous and inaccurate to say that this could have happened to anybody; some people are innately gifted with adult caution. Still, as I look back upon the mixture of bravado and naïveté—the absolute assurance that we could do no harm to ourselves—of the children who filled Geoffrey's truck that night, eager for any wildness he could deliver, I have no doubt that any one of us might have been captain of our own disaster.

TEN

In front of 1313 Third Avenue, my first
New York home, March 1976.

The darkness deepened and, making full use of new
liquor laws that lowered the legal drinking age to eighteen,
I consecrated most of the following year to alcohol—weird
stuff like Pernod, green Chartreuse, and a briefly available
tan liqueur called Damiana, which was sold in a bottle
shaped like the torso of a pregnant woman and made anybody who tried it crazy for the duration. Every morning I'd
wake up trembling, gag down a beer, smoke the first of the
day's four dozen unfiltered cigarettes, hack and sputter like
an old car coming apart, then walk to the Campus Restaurant, where I'd spike my coffee with shots of Kahlúa and
reread Malcolm Lowry or Arthur Rimbaud until it was

time to hit the bars. I always needed to escape myself, and this was the only period in my life that I was a dawn-to-dusk drinker, for the panic attacks would set in the moment the booze wore off.

I had now dropped out of high school, and somehow, between gulps, I managed to work part-time in a record store, The Disc, where I became the very model of the snide know-it-all counterperson we have all met and loathed—"Why are you buying *that*? They're a *horrible* group!" and so on. I was warned to stop lecturing the customers, and then warned again. After that, I was quickly fired, but not before I had secured a ninety-dollar-a-month lease on a tiny trailer in a park on the edge of campus.

Weeks Trailer Park was nothing to look at—it resembled a train wreck, cars tossed about scattershot—but I have an abiding affection for the place. Most of the trailers (nobody would have called these heaps "mobile homes") were at least twenty years old and eroding rapidly; they were propped up on piles of bricks, and the usual method of warming them was with combustible and illegal oil space heaters, lit by a long piece of burning newspaper. The water tasted like pond specimen, and the Board of Health was continually threatening to shut the whole place down for one reason or another. But there was a harmonious spirit there that year, with doors left unlocked and impromptu hippie parties at which anyone was welcome. As my home was just a two- or three-minute walk from both the high school and the Campus Restaurant, friends would drop by between classes. And it was autumn, always my most con-genial season, and I felt as though I were starting over.

Best of all, I had a girlfriend. Her name was Jennifer and we'd known each other for years, had even played together as children. Now, in a very short time, we set up housekeeping, and the few weeks that we had before things went sour were the happiest period of my adolescence. I stayed sober during the day, wrote poetry, and tried to compose; Jennifer sang and made pottery. She was a font of patience and practical sense, teaching me to button my shirts from bottom to top, so as not to forever misalign them (the formula had never occurred to me), and how to cook a few simple meals, some of which I still make today. I finally had the opportunity to grow accustomed to another person's body, and that closeness brought me sustained comfort instead of the usual rushing, panicked excitement. Our days were quiet and unhurried, and we entwined tightly in our single bed on the colder nights.

And then we had a fight, and nothing was ever the same. It always astonishes me how quickly and irrevocably relationships can break off, once their time has come; everything thought permanent collapses all at once, like the Soviet Union. Splitting up in a small town is especially painful, because the mating pool is so limited. Come Saturday night, it was a safe bet that I would run into the newly single Jennifer at Rapp's, and it was more than likely that she would eventually end up going out with one of my friends.

I cried for days when she left—sobbed convulsively, really, in heaving oceanic surges, and not just for Jenny but for Jon and Steve, for Mrs. Callahan and the woods off Washtenaw, for Mabel Normand and Geraldine Farrar, for passenger pigeons and vanished films, for Harry Hannah and the embers of Gold Hall, for the calming warmth my mother's lullabies had once bestowed, for the cold isolation that remained, for the boy I had been, for the man I felt so wretchedly equipped to become, for everything that was ephemeral, misplaced, and broken.

When I finally lifted myself from my bed, drained and purged, my eyes set back in a puffy scarlet orb, I was visited by one of those moments of strange clarity that occasionally follow trauma. I suddenly knew, with all my heart, that I did not want to have survived Hunting Lodge Road only to destroy myself anyway, and I made a sudden, steely determination to get well, no matter what it took. (Think of Scarlett O'Hara in her carrot patch and you'll have the general idea.) I gave away a half pack of cigarettes spontaneously and never smoked another. I cut back further on my drinking, and discovered, to my innocent surprise, that many of my panic attacks had sprung directly from hangovers. Finally, at the urging of a recently enlightened friend, I attended an introductory class in Transcendental Meditation.

The lecture was awful—a prim, suspiciously clean-cut young man drew diagrams on the blackboard, purporting to depict thoughts rising "like bubbles in a pond"—and I almost walked out. But I had already put down the sixty dollars it cost to learn the technique, which sounded exotic and otherworldly—it was even Beatles and Beach Boys-approved—so I stuck around.

My mother drove me to the Student Union on the cold,

clear morning that I learned to meditate, for I had been too nervous to walk there by myself. For much of my life, and especially since the accident, I had been robot-gaited, hunched up like Frankenstein, all muscles taut. But within seconds after I received my mantra—a secret word that you repeat to yourself and then permit to recur in your mind—my shoulders dropped automatically, something I wouldn't have been able to accomplish on my own had I worked on it for hours. Indeed, so much anxiety was released during that first twenty-minute meditation that I shocked my mother by walking back, for the sheer joy of moving comfortably, at home on the planet.

In the three and a half decades since, I have missed only a few days of meditation. For me, there is no discipline involved; this is something I love, both a vacation from and a reaffirmation of myself. During meditation, my mind is calm and alert, my heartbeat slows; I feel a subtle, distinct, and pleasurable tingling throughout my body, and I invariably emerge refreshed. I was never interested in progressing further in the direction of Eastern philosophy—or, for that matter, in the TM movement itself—but the technique has proved invaluable, and I count February 1, 1975, as one of my few private anniversaries that is purely celebratory.

I was now twenty years old, beginning to regain my health after its long battering from cigarettes and liqueur, and newly fortified with meditation. It had been more than a year since I had passed my high-school equivalency test, and it seemed time to ponder what might happen next. Pushing me along, gently but urgently, my mother sent me back to Tanglewood, where summer classes offered by Boston University had occasionally led to full matriculation at the home campus.

In Lenox, I moved into a sort of rental commune called the Music Inn, an improbable compound with a restaurant, a bar, a movie theater, and rooms for a hundred dollars a month—all just down the street from the Tanglewood Lion Gate. My apartment was in the same building as the movie house, Toad Hall, which showed revivals and cult classics— it was like living in an endless Friday Film Series—and I became friends with the proprietor, Richard Schwarz, who let me attend as often as I wanted so long as I sold popcorn before the shows.

The Music Inn had a tradition of outdoor concerts that dated back at least to the Modern Jazz Quartet and the live recordings it made on the premises in the 1950s. By the summer of 1975, caravans of young people from all over New York and New England found their way across the Massachusetts Turnpike to Lenox every weekend, for Saturdays of Frisbee-playing, wine-drinking, sun-soaking, and listening to music. That August, Bruce Springsteen had finished his *Born to Run* album and was preparing for the New York Bottom Line engagement that would help him win simultaneous cover stories in *Time* and *Newsweek* and introduce his work to a vast new audience. For two weeks in a row, he appeared at the Music Inn, literally in my backyard, where a couple hundred of us cheered him on; he reciprocated by playing for hours and hours.

Up at Tanglewood, I continued to sit toward the back of class, not at all convinced that my panic attacks were a thing of the past. My teacher, Leonard Altman, a compassionate man in his mid-fifties, watched me glide silently in and out of his classroom at the Hawthorne studio, and one day he asked me to stay after for a few minutes. "You look so terribly nervous out there," he said once we were alone, not realizing that his invitation had tripled my anxiety. "Is everything all right?"

It was thus that I met my most significant mentor. Leonard had run a classical-music magazine, a publishing company, a public-television program, and was then directing the music division of the New York State Council on the Arts. He had helped save Carnegie Hall from the wrecker's ball and had then gone on to lead a less successful fight to save the old Met. He had known Leonard Bernstein since their shared Boston childhoods, and was full of stories about other musicians and conductors: Vladimir Horowitz, Leopold Stokowski, and that Berkshires deity of deities, Serge Koussevitzky, who had founded Tanglewood during his tenure as music director of the Boston Symphony Orchestra.

And now he was my friend: this kindly, sophisticated, and worldly man with his extraordinary history actually saw something in me and was willing to help me find my way. "You won't believe this, but I think you are a natural New Yorker," Leonard told me over hamburgers on the screen porch of the Heritage House in Lenox, where generations of musicians had gathered through the decades. I replied that I never thought I'd be able to summon the courage to visit New York again, let alone live there. But he prevailed, and a couple of weeks later, after Tanglewood had adjourned and I was back in Storrs, dismayed by the prospect of another year of four-square Elton John hits on the Campus Restaurant's wobbly jukebox, I rode nervously down to Manhattan with my friend Bruce Reynolds.

It was the end of summer, and New York was pretty close to its all-time nadir. The city was going broke; murders were so commonplace that they hardly made the news; the South Bronx was burning night and day; Columbia University was seriously evaluating the pros and cons of a move to New Jersey; and a July strike had left acrid ramparts of garbage lining even the fanciest avenues. You did not walk the streets of Greenwich Village so much as play hopscotch down them, to avoid sliding in dog droppings. Under such circumstances, the fact that we were able to book a double room at the Waldorf Astoria at a student rate of thirty dollars was not remarkable, although newer New Yorkers may be startled to learn that it was ever possible to use the words "Waldorf Astoria" and "student rate" in the same sentence.

That first night, Bruce and I both wanted steak, so we called Manny Wolf's, a place that also had a branch near Tanglewood. A gentleman answered the phone, and I asked him in all seriousness what were the odds that we would be mugged while walking to the restaurant. "Well, you're at the Waldorf, at Forty-ninth and Park, and we're at Forty-ninth and Third," he replied as patiently as possible. "It's still light out, you're both grown men, and I can pretty much say with a hundred-percent surety that you won't be mugged." Indeed, we survived, and in the two blocks to the restaurant we saw many thousands of people—glamorous and dynamic women striding by like long, sharp scissors—seemingly all doing fine, carrying on their lives without recognizable fear and trembling. I began to smile.

Leonard met us for lunch the next day and suggested that I apply to a school I'd never heard of, the Mannes College of Music. He had already called the dean and been assured that Mannes would welcome me as an unclassified student. My mother, by now convinced that Leonard was heaven-sent, agreed immediately to set me up in Manhattan, which called for nothing like the massive investment that would be required a few years later. And so, in less than two weeks, everything was settled; I would go to Mannes, and right away. I felt like an arrow that had been pulled back for twenty years, finally released to speed toward a target.

And so I joined the thousands of young people who flocked to New York in the mid-seventies, defying the crime, the decay, and the warnings of parents, teachers, and social scientists who promised us the game was over. I didn't know whether I had a future, but I wanted no more of my past, and the city, with its hummingbird-heart vitality, its supreme indifference, offered abrupt and certain change.

A curious face-blindness affected me in those first few weeks: I was always stopping pedestrians in the crowd, thinking that I recognized them from Storrs. I'd shout, "Hey, Peter! It's Tim Page!," and a stranger would stare back at me as though I were crazy. My powers of observation weren't at all well tuned; in Storrs, there had been so few faces to know that anybody who looked remotely like somebody was surely that person. Now I was in a city with millions of faces, and it wasn't always a comfortable transition. But whenever I experienced some passing physical panic I'd shut my eyes, start to meditate, and the fear would subside. For the more general everyday angst, Leonard's telephone had an answering machine—a rarity back then—with a wonderfully reassuring message: "I'm sorry I missed your call, but I'll make sure to call you just as soon as I get back, and that shouldn't be very long from now." *"That shouldn't be very long from now"*—how many times did that phrase keep me afloat! If I could only hold on for a few more hours, Leonard would call and things would surely be better.

Mannes, a warm, intimate, European-style conservatory, was then located in four old town houses on East Seventy-fourth Street. I was blunt with my teachers about my conviction that I was doomed to fail, and they tempered their professional rigor with countless acts of personal kindness. My major was composition, and I was accepted as a student by Charles Jones.

He was always *Mister* Jones. I never thought he would actually have minded it if we called him Charles, particularly once we had grown out of our apprenticeship and into what passed for full maturity. But something about his presence, gracious and supportive as he invariably was, prompted an adherence to old-world manners. Mr. Jones he was—and, as far as I'm concerned, Mr. Jones he will remain.

Those of us who were fortunate enough to have called him our teacher would make our way to 311 East Fifty-eighth Street down Second Avenue or, perhaps, wander over from the subway stop above Bloomingdale's. Confronted with what still seems a fairy-tale house, we would unlatch the picket fence (in midtown Manhattan!), ring a loud, old-fashioned doorbell, and suddenly Mr. Jones would appear in his smoking jacket, ushering us into his living room, greeting us, artist to artist—"Ah, yes! Come in, come in . . ."

How many others among his students date their artistic coming-of-age to those late winter afternoons seated at Mr. Jones's Steinway? Our meetings would combine aesthetic advice, score reading, historical analysis, delicious anecdotes, and near-parental warmth, for he was always aware of just how lonely New York City could be for a newcomer.

I would arrive intoxicated on Philip Glass one week, on Olivier Messiaen the next, and on the *Four Last Songs* of Richard Strauss the week following. He would listen to what I had prepared (pretty eclectic stuff in those days!), size up its strengths and weaknesses, and make suggestions that were invariably both encouraging and of immense practical help. Even when he actively disliked the works of a given composer (Shostakovich and Sibelius were two long-standing—and at least partly generational—bêtes noires), he always retained a keen interest in the reasons that his students had somehow taken to this dreadful music.

In short, Mr. Jones was a thoughtful, creative, and stimulating guide, amazingly generous with his time and his friendship. He seemed to know everybody—at one East Fifty-eighth Street party, I recall scanning the room and spotting most of the old guard of American composers:

Roger Sessions, Elliott Carter, Vittorio Rieti, Virgil Thomson, and Ned Rorem—and he always made sure that his pupils were introduced all around.

My shyness persisted, however, and I had only two friends at Mannes that freshman year—a pianist and composer named Fred Patella, with whom I ate four-dollar lunches, complete with beer, in one or another of the little German restaurants that once lined East Eighty-sixth Street; and Vivian King, a clarinet player from North Carolina with an absolutely impenetrable Southern accent who lived downstairs from me. Both had left the school by the following fall, and I found myself in that very strange but all too common New York dilemma of being surrounded by masses of people and knowing almost nobody. I forced myself to go to the Mannes Student Lounge and, hard as it was, to strike up a conversation with a different stranger every day. At last I found a working formula for making friends: Mannes had only two hundred students then and one introduction made for another, and after two or three weeks I knew almost everyone in the school.

I had found a foothold in this new life, and I was grateful. Still, as I settled into Manhattan, I quickly decided that I was more interested in writing prose than in writing music. My blithe explanation in years to come would be that I was a good enough critic to recognize that I wasn't a good enough composer, but in fact I like a few of the pieces I wrote. Their creation came slowly, however—a few measures of music from an afternoon's labor—and it seemed practical to work with words instead, where I was much more fluent.

And so I took a summer writing course at Columbia University, as a first step toward transferring to the college. In those days, Columbia was an intensely intellectual and rather chilly place. But I wanted that coldness, that sense of solemn, unsentimental cerebration, and I felt ready for it. Our assignment was to produce a five-hundred-word essay every night, and I took the challenge personally, writing on such disparate topics as the unjust imprisonment of Patty Hearst, my disappointment with the Beach Boys' worst album, *15 Big Ones,* and my favorite Spanish restaurant in the Village. My final project was a three-thousand-word analysis of *Face to Face,* one of Ingmar Bergman's least successful films (it would be one of three that he specifically disowned), but the first that I'd been able to see time and time again, as it ran for more than a month at the Beekman Theater on Second Avenue.

But I date my first more or less mature criticism to the world premiere of Steve Reich's *Music for 18 Musicians,* which I heard in New York at the Town Hall in April of 1976. I climbed the five flights to my Third Avenue walkup, knowing that I'd never fall asleep, with an urgent need to *react,* in some concrete and personal manner, to the work. If I had been a dancer, I might have danced it; if I had been a filmmaker, I might have plotted a film to it. As a would-be writer, I had to try and write it.

So I went to the typewriter and started to free-associate, gradually zeroing in on the images that came to mind. What I had heard struck me as so opulent and unusual, so distinctly of its time but in such radical opposition to most "new music" of the seventies, that I wrote through the night, attempting to summarize my impressions. Five years later, I published a study of what by then had come to be known as minimalism, and it incorporated some of what I wrote that night:

> Minerva-like, the music springs to life fully
> formed—from dead silence to fever pitch.
> There is a strong feeling of ritual, a sense that
> on some subliminal plane the music has always
> been playing and that it will continue playing
> forever. . . . Imagine concentrating on a
> challenging modern painting that becomes just
> a little different every time you shift your
> attention from one detail to another. Or trying
> to impose a frame on a running river—making
> it a finite, enclosed work of art yet leaving its
> kinetic quality unsullied, leaving it flowing
> freely on all sides. It has been done. Steve Reich
> has framed the river.

Today, I find myself wondering if I would have responded so profoundly to this starkly reiterative, rigidly patterned music had I not had Asperger's syndrome. This is not an aesthetic cop-out: I can make an intellectual case for minimalism, and I am hardly the only writer who has done so. But its initial appeal for me was purely visceral. As the Quakers might say, this music spoke to my condition; it was what my insides sounded like. (I would later experience a similar, curiously mechanical limbic ecstasy upon a first encounter with *Last Year at Marienbad*.)

It is easy to feel nostalgic for those years in New York, and not only because I was so much younger. Manhattan was a different city then. Rents were stable, the clubs were cheap and stayed open late, nobody dressed up or down, and even the hardships seemed romantic. In the fall of 1976, I attended the American premiere of the Philip Glass–Robert Wilson opera *Einstein on the Beach* at the Metropolitan Opera, transfixed in my seat for the full five-hour duration and then staying on to whoop and cheer until I was all but ejected from the building. (How astonished I would have been to learn that I would serve as a copyist for Glass's next opera, *Satyagraha*, and that this great and good man would befriend me.) The following year, I was accepted into Columbia and moved to a Riverside Drive apartment that would be mine for the next two decades. I helped my Toad Hall movie buddy Richard Schwarz renovate and reopen the Upper West Side's antiquated revival house, the Thalia. I joined WKCR, Columbia's radio station, and soon had a weekly show, to which I invited composers and musicians I admired, thus setting into motion what would turn out to be my career. And, like so many who make the move from a small town to a big city, I became an insufferable snob for a while.

When speaking of Storrs, even—perhaps especially—to people who lived there, I would mimic the poet and composer Philip Heseltine, who once summed up a bucolic Vaughan Williams symphony by comparing it to a cow looking over a fence: "It's very beautiful—and so what?" It's not quite true that Manhattanites are the most provincial people in the world, but only a member of that clan would have offered the awkward compliment I paid to my dentist in an affluent Connecticut suburb after he had worked on my teeth: "You're doing so well here—when do you think you'll try to make it in New York?" I was stunned when he told me that he liked it just fine in West Hartford and had no plans whatsoever to move. Such closed-mindedness, I thought!—not recognizing any of this in myself.

One of the things I now dislike most about Manhattan— the need to don some sort of psychological armor to make it through the day—was liberating to me then. In Storrs, almost everything you saw was explainable; every narrative, once commenced, could likely be followed to an end. But New York was an onslaught of dissociated stimuli, jarring and exhilarating. I quickly learned that I couldn't give to every panhandler, no matter how sad the story; I couldn't keep track of all the dramas on the street, and I had to laugh off rudeness and aggression. As such, by necessity I managed to close off most of my receptors. This emotional shield, which becomes habitual and which I have since tried very hard to purge from my system, permitted and even encouraged me to ignore whatever was going on around me, and for a time I grew purely selfish, as though nothing else existed but a few chosen people and my goals.

And so I stayed—adrift and awash, trying on parts, dreamy, decadent poet one day, ambitious young-man-in-a-hurry the next. I slept on the roof of my building on torrid summer nights and in wintertime shivered outside ephemeral nightclubs under the glare of fish-faced doormen with painted hair. I shared pitchers of beer with third-party candidates, writers who never wrote, oh-so-hip bohemians who claimed to have known Thomas Pynchon at Cornell, and hungry young actresses who boasted of their "contacts" while making it clear that I would never, ever be among them. To my astonishment, I thrived in New York and several weeks might pass without a crisis. I began to turn down the third pitcher and go to bed early. And some of the furies began to burn away.

Paul Moore: "It must be nice to always believe you know better, to always think you're the smartest person in the room."
Jane Craig: "No, it's awful."

—James L. Brooks, *Broadcast News*

Clifford Pyncheon: "It is late! I want my happiness!"

—Nathaniel Hawthorne,
The House of the Seven Gables

EPILOGUE

Cub reporter: *SoHo News.* 1979.

One evening in 1979, a few weeks out of college and thoroughly confused about the future, I walked downstairs into a Greenwich Village store and purchased Pierre Boulez's new recording of the complete music of Anton Webern. I took it home, listened to it, loved it, and then spent three days distilling my excitement into words. When I finished, I sent the article, unsolicited, to the *SoHo Weekly News,* a brightly hedonistic, determinedly avant-garde arts magazine that was then published in lower Manhattan.

I had no friends at the *SoHo News,* no reason to believe that its editors would want my thoughts on this particular subject. (Then, as now, dissertations on Webern were not exactly hot property.) But my story was accepted, published, and even paid for, after a month or two and some prodding on my part. And suddenly I was a music critic. That was my primary job until the end of 2007—at the *SoHo News,* the *New York Times, Newsday,* and, ultimately, the *Washington Post*—and I reserve the right to return to it on occasion, in much the same spirit that I revisit Storrs. Since 1979, I have also written and edited books, mostly on creative figures I find intriguing (the novelists Dawn Powell and Sigrid Undset, the agnostic nineteenth-century "preacher" Robert Green Ingersoll, the pianists William Kapell and Glenn Gould, the last of whom became a friend). I have been involved in any number of radio and recording projects, and I have lately discovered that I love to teach.

It has been my extraordinary good fortune to find work that makes use of my strengths and doesn't test my weaknesses. To this day, if you put me behind a busy sales counter, a meltdown would be imminent, for I can't easily read new faces and shifting attention rapidly from one unfamiliar person to another overwhelms me. If I could choose to have one supernatural power, it would undoubtedly be invisibility, and yet I want and need public acknowledgment of my work. I suffer little stage fright when it comes to public speaking or appearances on radio or television—I've got those particular acts figured out—but unstructured participation in social gatherings remains agonizing, unless I know exactly what is expected from me. It would be easier for me to improvise an epic poem before a sellout crowd at Madison Square Garden than to approach an attractive stranger across the room and strike up a conversation.

I had a real slapping-down when I took a senior administrative position at the St. Louis Symphony Orchestra, where I worked with a hundred musicians and a staff of about twenty-five, almost all of them very nice people indeed. But I was a disaster. There were numerous extra-musical facets of the job that didn't interest me and to which I couldn't pay attention. Not wouldn't, *couldn't*. Any sort of prevarication—even a harmless official compliment after a less than stellar performance—was foreign to me, and I was unable to keep state secrets. Nor was I politic with donors; I'm afraid I laughed out loud when one trustee suggested that we'd sell more tickets if we put Ravel's *Bolero* on every program, but I had thought, for a few seconds, that she was joking.

In the summer of 2000, I resigned from the St. Louis Symphony, limped away from the Midwest, and settled outside Washington. I hadn't been so depressed since just after the accident in Storrs, and I decided to go back into therapy. One psychiatrist concluded that I was bipolar and put me on lithium, which did nothing but make me feel weirdly outsized, as though my body stretched up miles from the ground, like a Giacometti figure. Another doctor suggested a new anti-anxiety medication, which I duly added to the clutter of bottles by my bedside. And then, after a series of family consultations, a New York psychologist named Keith Westerfield surprised me first with a thoughtful explanation and then with a formal diagnosis of Asperger's syndrome.

I bought a book of essays on the condition, edited by Ami Klin, Fred R. Volkmar, and Sara S. Sparrow, and devoured it with stunned fascination. Despite the daunting medical language of some of the chapters, I felt as though I had stumbled upon my secret biography. Here it all was—the computer-like retention, the physical awkwardness, the difficulties with peers and lovers, the need for routine and repetition, the narrow, specialized interests (one article even mentioned silent film, old recordings, and true crime—had they created a developmental disorder just for me?). I was forty-five years old when I learned that I wasn't alone.

Every so often, someone asks if I would undergo some yet-to-be-discovered treatment that might end my Asperger's syndrome. Such questions have become politically fraught, and my answer is a complicated one. I wouldn't wish the condition on anybody—I've spent too much of my life isolated, unhappy, and conflicted—yet I am also convinced that many of the things I've done were accomplished not despite my Asperger's syndrome but *because* of it. I'm sure that it's responsible, at least in part, for my powers of concentration, which permit me to absorb a congenial subject immediately, write an article in an afternoon or a book in a summer, blotting out everyone and everything until the project is completed. I'm sure that it's one of the reasons I take my work so seriously (I find it far easier to forgive any sort of personal insult than the slightest outside meddling with a project that has seized my attention—do not disturb my circles!). And I wouldn't swap my sensory melding of music and words for anything, for it continues to provide me with a privileged and other-worldly ecstasy into my sixth decade.

Nevertheless, my strangeness persists and I know that there is a lot that simply slips by. I can have lunch with somebody and come away with no memory of what she was wearing. I still neglect my shirttails, my shoelaces, and, on rare and embarrassing occasions, my zipper. If someone were to ask me to close my eyes right now and describe the clothes I had on today, I would have to think hard about it and might well answer incorrectly.

One of the things everybody "knows" about people on the autistic spectrum is that we have difficulty looking other people in the eye. This happens to be a behavioral pattern that I have mastered, something my father demanded from such an early age that I inculcated the habit, and can brazen my way through eye-to-eye contact easily, an actor playing his part. Yet I invariably look away when speaking of anything that moves me deeply. Moreover, although I've had a prescription for eyeglasses for the past twenty years, I'm most comfortable not wearing them. I used to put them on only to review opera, when I felt that I owed my readers some description of what might be happening on the stage. But I rarely wear my glasses now, for they make me aware of too much. All of a sudden, it feels as though I've been cast into a world of strangers, all staring at me, so clear and so close that I'm flooded by the intimacy. Far more comfortable to drift along in a haze, an oblivious dormouse. Myopia makes for handy insulation; I don't need glasses to read, and I can still see well enough to gaze across a table and safely admire the face of a trusted dinner companion.

This elected nearsightedness is possible only because I have remained a nondriver. For years after the accident, I was a jumpy passenger and would flinch the moment I perceived any deviation, however fleeting, from the center of the road. Thereafter I moved to New York, where car ownership was not only unnecessary but a major bother. Today, I feel rather too old a dog to learn this particular trick, and the very idea of entering into the sort of aggressive personal competition that I observe on the road is inconceivable to me. And so, at some sacrifice to my own and others' convenience, I have managed to avoid learning to drive, despite the fact that the prospect of immediate escape from places and situations remains essential to my emotional well-being. As such, I limit myself mostly to cities, where I can call a cab or jump on public transportation if I need to get away—a need that comes on strongly and suddenly.

Overstimulation of any sort remains a positive horror, and I am most content either alone, with people I have known a long time, or with the occasional new friend I make and love instantly, as though we were born together. I generally prefer dark or neutral clothing and gray skies, but I make conspicuous exceptions for both Caracas and California, where, for whatever unfathomable reason, the sun feels right. Wherever I am, I like to walk into the same restaurants, sit in the same seats, and order the same meals, and I took personal offense when New York's Pan Am Building began passing itself off as MetLife.

Some people make me crazy—pushing their faces into

mine, finishing my sentences, repeatedly calling my attention to things that don't interest me and that I don't care to know about—and I can take these distractions for only a short time before I become unhappy and, on occasion, downright rude. In such circumstances, I feel physically threatened, as though I were trapped in an astronaut suit and somebody had released a hornet into the helmet, where it buzzes in my ear, stings my nose, and beats its wings against my eyelids and there is no way to smack or even deflect it.

I accept Romain Rolland's practical credo—"pessimism of the intelligence; optimism of the will"—as a guide to my possibilities. I've transcended Harry Lauder and horehound drops, and my passions now range widely, if spottily, through any number of fields. Laughter, meditation, therapy, antidepressants, Valium, liberal helpings of wine and beer, loyal and patient friends, forgiving children, a congenial work situation that allows me to spend much of my time by myself—all these have helped me to carry on. I've also grown less rigid over the years. Aggressively stupid expressions of optimism, such as the song "Bluebird of Happiness" or the film *Forrest Gump,* used to send me into a fury; now I just marvel at the many responses to the human condition and how different they are from my own. For some of us, stories where the characters *don't* live happily ever after, where the hero is too late to save the day, where nothing is redeemed, are curiously restorative, for they present a vision of the world that serves to reinforce what we see with our own eyes, and the truth isn't so terrible that it can't be told.

By now, of course, I am fairly used to myself and my symptoms bloom publicly only on rare occasions. Waiting for the check after a Washington lunch in 2005, I realized that it was both the hundred and fortieth anniversary of Lincoln's assassination and exactly forty years since the murderers of the Clutter family (*In Cold Blood*) were put to death in Kansas. I doubt that my companion was equally thrilled by this coincidence, especially when elaborated upon in such sudden, bursting detail in the middle of a glorious spring day, but at least I controlled the temptation to launch into a lengthy examination of the culpability of Mrs. Surratt. I count that as progress.

The fact that my understanding of affection, comradeship, and human empathy has been hard-won rather than hardwired from the start does not make those feelings less genuine. I remain friends with most of the people I was friends with thirty years ago, and I worry about them daily (here I concur with Virgil Thomson, who said that worry was one form of prayer he deemed acceptable). My intimates, new and old, are permanent fixtures in my experience, and the fact that some of them—too many—are no longer living has not diminished my devotion.

When I was twenty-nine years old, I realized that it was probably time to get married; the decision, I'm sorry to say, was just as cold-blooded and pragmatic as that. I married my best friend, a brilliant and intuitive woman, someone I admired and cared for and to whom I felt and feel enormous loyalty. But my capacity for intimacy was then very limited and the marriage lingered but couldn't last. Our best moments were the births—gory, violent, and spectacularly beautiful—of our three sons, when I held on to one of her legs, mopped her brow, gave whatever comfort I could, and eventually cried for joy as a brand-new child was laid on her belly. How I pity my father—and his father and most Western fathers back to the beginning of the modern world—so long excluded from these astounding communions!

Thereafter, I learned to burp babies and grew adept with a diaper. And yet I know that I was not as responsive a father to little William, Robert, and John as I would have liked to be. Overwrought and preoccupied at home, I traveled whenever I could. A music festival once offered me expenses and a hundred-dollar honorarium to spend a whole week in a Midwestern Holiday Inn, and I accepted immediately, just to find some solitude and calm myself down, the very same reason that I used to flee to the nurse's office.

The relationship with my children has grown closer as we've all grown up; I love them, they fascinate me, and I am never happier than when one or more of them is visiting. But I shy away from extensive involvement in their day-to-day lives, which continues to feel unnatural. Perhaps I had to fight off too much intrusion from my father. Then again, as I sometimes fear, perhaps I am not quite a mammal.

My own parents were affected by dementia for several years before they died. My mother's experience was hellish; whenever her caretakers prepared her for a bath, she seemed to think that she was being violated and her shrieks were piteous. But some of my father's most agreeable days occurred after he was deep into Alzheimer's. During his long Indian summer, my sister and I would regularly take him out to dinner with his grandchildren, and he'd drink half a glass of wine and spend the rest of the evening beaming at us—not knowing our names, perhaps, but surely grasping our essence—with a show of unguarded affection that he was never able to permit himself when younger. He had overvalued the intellect all his life, and I suspect that he was almost grateful that it left him alone at the end.

By then, it was the twenty-first century and I had fallen in love, which astonished me. I had never imagined sustained contentment, and certainly not in the company of another person. Yet here it was: even making the bed together in the morning, an act that had hitherto struck me as Sisyphean, took on meaning, as the prelude to another gloriously ordinary day, to be followed by tea, the newspapers, a couple of hours of work, and then lunch in the neighborhood. While it lasted, everything was enhanced; the only thing I can compare it to is that moment when *The Wizard of Oz* turns from black and white into color.

She wanted a life commitment and was determined to win me over. I resisted as long as I could, for my sense of self-protection was too strong—and if I let her in, what could I ever do if she went away? But I found myself invaded, physically and emotionally, and, for the first time in my life, I was ready for it. Thereafter, I considered any day not spent with her a day diminished. I was no longer a scared kid being taken to bed but a full and eager partner, and I lived for several years in a constant state of amazed and grateful surprise. Gasping awake after yet another nightmare that I couldn't remember, I would bury my face in her back, acclimate myself to her steady breathing, and fall asleep again, at peace for a while.

We bought a house in Baltimore and chose a quotation from H. L. Mencken to hang in our front hall:

> A home is not a mere transient shelter: its essence lies in its permanence, in its capacity for accretion and solidification, in its quality of representing, in all its details, the personalities of the people who live in it. In the course of years it becomes a sort of museum of these people; they give it its indefinable air, separating it from all other homes, as one human face is separated from all others. It is at once a refuge from the world, a treasure-house, a castle, and the shrine of a whole hierarchy of peculiarly private and potent gods.

And then, suddenly and without warning, she had to leave and she was too regretful or too solitary or maybe simply too compassionate to tell me why. And I became a crazy man, so stunned and shocked that I felt mortally wounded. I'd finally found a mate—somebody I liked, loved, respected, admired, and lusted for all at once. Now I was alone again. I couldn't comprehend what had happened, and whenever I believed it, even for a moment, the pain was unbearable.

I thought constantly of our honeymoon, so soon before—of the delighted energy in her eyes as she prepared to take a sunrise train out of Edinburgh to play golf at St. Andrew's, to return home glistening with endorphins and cold Scottish rain. I felt her presence everywhere; even the discovery of something as trivial as a restaurant receipt once used as a bookmark led to a stream of associations that I would follow unto madness. If the receipt was dated, say, December 5, 2004, I'd immediately do the math, reflect that we had then been married for a little over two years and still had almost another two to go before the world ended. And I'd wonder, for the thousandth futile, stupid, brain-numbing time, whether something, somehow, might have been saved had I said or done something *right then.*

Far better to become obsessed with projects than with people, I had always believed, and this loss seemed to confirm it. After all, when you have finished writing a book or making a record, you can read it or listen to it, put it on a shelf or give it to a friend—it is a palpable accomplishment that cannot be taken away from you, not entirely. Still, when the time came to pick myself up, as after a death, I made it a deliberate, desperate point to go out on as many dates as possible, where I met attractive people and made at least one permanent friend. Today, becalmed, I can only be grateful for what I once had, which is a lot more than some people are allowed, and a blessing that I nearly missed.

I stayed in Baltimore, where I live in a 1900 row house built for a marble importer, with samplings of his wares throughout, down to the kitchen and the bathrooms. A century ago, for about ten years, mine was the most fashionable neighborhood in town. Then came the craze for backyards and side windows—"Aren't you tired of living in a tunnel?" the developers inveigled—and the money moved up to Guilford or Roland Park or out to the suburbs and the golden age of the Baltimore row house came to an end.

Those impractical old palaces remain wonderful places to live and, after the financial humiliations and space constraints that New York and Washington inflict on anyone without an endless surfeit of cash, I was startled to learn that I could afford one of them. When I arrived in Baltimore, it was said to be the last large city in America where the drummer in a punk band could own his own house. Another friend described it as "a city of great bars and scary walks back to the car." I can attest to the great bars and I am not oblivious to Baltimore's problems, but, paradoxically, I've never encountered another place where casual, day-to-day encounters with one's neighbors are likely to be so courteous and friendly. Baltimore may be a dangerous place—our police blotter attests to that—but, in my experience, it is also a curiously accepting and gentle-tempered one, and those of us who like the city at all tend to love it.

Until recently, Baltimore had been losing population for half a century and various official slogans were adopted to try to reverse the trend. First there was "Baltimore: The City that Reads" (it doesn't—at least not as much as Boston, San Francisco, and a hundred other places). Then there was "Baltimore: The Greatest City in America" (the *greatest*? Much of Baltimore's attraction has to do with its easy comforts and near-dowdy modesty—it is the *anti*-Manhattan and we like it that way). Lately, there has been "Baltimore: Get In on It!," which sounds like a cynical invitation to a real-estate fire sale. If there must be a catchphrase, the best suggestion I've heard is "Baltimore: Be Yourself." That's good advice anywhere, but it perfectly suits what may be the most hospitable city for eccentrics and individualists between London and San Francisco.

Aspies are predetermined individualists—people both condemned and liberated to live in our own worlds—but, after a while, if we can summon up the courage, we stop apologizing for it. The most diverse and unexpected things bring me delight, not just Bergman and Berlioz and established masterpieces but the nineteenth-century Dutch painter Emile van Marcke's numberless studies of tranquil cows gazing placidly from the ghosts of forests long paved over; out-of-date New York phone directories that tell where everybody lived before they became famous; friendly dogs to commune with on a kitchen floor; Three Stooges shorts, especially the ones with Curly in full mania; the way women martial artists move their bodies, all dance and devastation; Alvin Lucier's *I Am Sitting in a Room*, in which words become music, sound becomes shimmer, and a natural process of acoustics is demonstrated in the most elegant and ethereal fashion; the gigantic old neon figure of Felix the Cat lit up high above the Chevrolet dealer on Figueroa Street, dominating the skyline of south Los Angeles with a mixture of historical significance and crazy camp; the radiant music of Judee Sill, the short-lived singer-songwriter who created and perfected her own kind of hymns—guileless, urgent, naked, absolutely personal. Ask me again tomorrow, and I might come up with a completely different list.

And yet, even in this world so full of a number of things,

I am still gloomy and anxious much of the time—more so, in some ways, than when I was young. Life is slipping away, I am aware of my own decay, and I have reached the point where every parting begins to feel permanent. Nights are particularly hard; I invariably wake up three or four hours after I go to bed, feeling clenched, badly oiled, and acutely aware of my own gravity. Although I am not particularly afraid of death unless I think I shall face it right away, I maintain a childlike horror of dying alone, and I am capable of turning 3 AM into a lugubrious opera of self-pity. What happens after death doesn't concern me much; I continue to have no formal religious beliefs and expect either an eternal, dreamless sleep or something so altogether extraordinary that no human brain could possibly comprehend it, let alone codify it and turn it into dogma. Small comfort before the pills kick in.

When I was younger, I used to collect the last words of the dying, even though I always suspected these were tidied up or romanticized in the retelling, and that the usual response to life's cessation is a groan, a curse, or wild confusion ("What's *this*?" Leonard Bernstein said as he fell back into eternity). There are brave and unreconciled final gasps of anger, such as Eugene O'Neill's "Born in a hotel room and now I'm dying in a goddamn hotel room!" There are sober, poignant epitaphs, such as the one offered by the man who was both our twenty-second and our twenty-fourth president, Grover Cleveland: "I have tried so hard to do right." And Aldous Huxley, who died on the same day as C. S. Lewis and John F. Kennedy (what would these three gentlemen have said to one another as they crossed the

Styx?), even managed to leave behind a last morsel of melancholy wisdom: "It is a bit embarrassing to have been concerned with the human problem all one's life and find at the end that one has no more to offer by way of advice than 'Try and be a little kinder.' "

So here are some "last words," on this clement August afternoon in the early twenty-first century, a day when much of the exhausted planet is still managing, if barely, to function for a little while longer. I am writing this in a Baltimore pub where the bartenders know me and I'm sort of the geezer-in-residence, sitting alone at a favorite table where I have done much to turn my liver into pâté, with the day's first pint of beer barely touched and at least two more to come, gazing contentedly through the picture window at the blurred figures of young people moving briskly up and down Charles Street.

Martha and the Vandellas are singing "Heat Wave" on the radio, as they always will, and I exult once more in the way the song's ultra-taut rhythms never constrict its jubilation. Baltimore's own summer torpor has finally broken, and tonight a welcome thunderstorm will drench the rats and rooftops of this old city. And I'm thinking back to the beginning of the summer, when I feared that I'd never complete this book, to the day when my friend Jennifer drove me to a beach in South Carolina. "Take off your shoes," she urged. "The sand is good for your feet, the water is warm, and you'll be walking in the ocean!" I rolled up my seersucker trousers and waded out into strangeness. At first, the sensations were too much for me and I recoiled. But the water *was* warm and the day was fine, its low-lying clouds purplish and pregnant with rain, and the receding tide distorted my footprints and then dragged them out to sea amid broken flecks of glittering shell. That struck me as funny and I laughed at the process, and in a while it was beautiful.

I have a mistrust of happy endings. Still, today—this hour—I am satisfied. Soon I will return to a house full of books, most of which I've read and some of which I created—a youthful dream fulfilled. There will be films to watch, there is music to listen to, there may be something to say. I know the maps of Mansfield and Ashford, but I have also explored far corners of London, Vienna, and Helsinki. I have climbed Mount Avila and gazed down on smoky Caracas, then out over the blue-green expanse of the Caribbean Sea, wind and tears in my face. I have been a lover and a father; I have learned to make and keep my friends. And if I am still something of a stranger in this world, a predestined outsider, I remain profoundly grateful for my life and its fitful and mysterious spells of invisible joy.

And now I am the author of *Parallel Play.*

Tim Page
The Brewer's Art
Baltimore, Maryland
August 23, 2008

ACKNOWLEDGMENTS

At home in Baltimore, 2008.

Parallel Play would never have come to pass without David Remnick, the editor of *The New Yorker,* who urged me to write about my experiences with Asperger's syndrome during a particularly low moment. All at once, I had a fresh adventure—something to explore—and the world took on renewed interest.

Ross Perlin traveled from breezy San Francisco to hot, humid Baltimore to work with me throughout June and July of 2008. He served as secretary, interrogator, psychologist, confessor, and the intellectual equivalent of a personal trainer, helping me to transform scattered shards into the beginning of a manuscript. My gratitude to this brilliant young man cannot be overstated, and I owe Katherine Stirling of *The New Yorker* heartfelt thanks for sending him my way.

My agent, Melanie Jackson, has seen me through ten books now, most of them pretty quixotic, yet she has never complained or tried to push me into any project, however lucrative, that didn't fit. All authors should have such a fierce, skillful, devoted, and high-minded advocate.

I owe debts to Phyllis Grann, my editor at Doubleday, and to Steve Rubin, Doubleday's past president and publisher, for their immediate enthusiasm for *Parallel Play*, their continuing encouragement, and all that they did to shape the finished volume. Jackie Montalvo, also at Doubleday, worked with me on the manuscript day after day as it progressed from first draft to completed book, and she has been cheerful, insightful, and of enormous help throughout.

Thanks to Vanessa Weeks Page and Julieta Stack, the two extraordinary women who took me on as husband for a while, and to my sons William Dean Page, Robert Leonard Page, and John Sherman Page, whom I love with all my heart. It was Julieta who came up with "Baltimore: Be Yourself." Vanessa has been reading my work critically for more than a quarter of a century now, and she has improved every page of this book.

Gary Bennett has been a sure and supportive friend for most of my life, and I owe him more than I can say. I am especially grateful to Jennifer Bellis, for her kindness, compassion, side-by-side meditations, and Folly Beach.

This book is dedicated in part to Philip Glass, with

thanks for thirty years of friendship and inspiration, both personal and creative.

Let me put in one good word for Valium, a restorative and much-maligned drug that I have been taking almost every day for more than thirty-five years and never found habit-forming. (Save the Dunesville monkeys!)

Further thanks to Elizabeth Aaron, Paul Alexander, Sasha Anawalt, Carol Anderson, Tony Attwood, Allison Lee Axinn, Meri Axinn, Susan Beers, Chuck Blanchard, Jennifer Bloomer, Dorothy Bognar, Helen Breasted and Peter Horton, Maude Bryt, John Buckley, Frank Busse, Amy Callahan, John Carini, Steve Carini, Mary Baird Carlsen, Jack and Louise Cawley, Katie Cawley, Jean Chapman, Louis Chatey, Tina Clarke, K. C. Cole, William A. Collins, John G. Connor, Tacy Cook, Ed Cray, Camilla Crossgrove, Cory Crossgrove, Roger Crossgrove, Donald and Bonnie Crosby, Andrew Curry, Justin Davidson and Ariella Budick, Bill Davis, Anna Lou Dehavenon, Lois Draegin, Gwen Duff, Jim Edinberg, Bob Fancher, Peter Fish, Michael Flynn, Sharon Francis, Jeffrey Frank, Gwendolyn Haverstock Freed, Arthur Gelb, James Glicker, Claudia Gonson, Donald E. Graham, Steve Gregoropoulos, Lynn Grenier, Larry Groff, Dudley and Wendy Duff Hamlin, Bev Harp, Paul Haskew, Deborah Heard, Jeffrey Herman, Christina Hinton, David Hoffman, Susan Hood, Thirza Hope, Polly Holliday, Anne Humphrey, Betsy and Mort Jaffe, Kay Redfield Jamison, Karen Johnson, Sally Jones, Robert G. Kaiser, David G. Kanzeg, Kerry Keddy, Nancy Utley Kelly, Robin Kline, Allan Kozinn, David Kraus, Hildie Kraus and Cam Gere, Alan M. and Sali Ann Kriegsman, Karen Kushner, Heather Brine

Lambert, Bea Liebenberg, Richard Leiby, Bill and Jean Lonergan, Clifford J. Lotz, Karyn Marcus, Erin McAleavy, Heather McGahee, Jerry Miller, Rob and Lesley Minearo, Karin Moody, Peter Occhiogrosso, Patrick O'Connor, Sean O'Hagan, Geneva Overholser, Franklin Reynolds Page, Pam Page, Richard and Jean Reynolds Page, John Pancake, Michael Parks, Fred Patella, Peter Perl, Gerald Perman, Jose Zugeber Pharmer, Arturo Pilar, Adam Clayton Powell III and Irene Solet, Leonard Press, Ronni J. Reich and Noah Stern Weber, David Reuben, Bruce and Raquel Reynolds, John Rockwell, Linda Volle Rogers, Norman Rosenthal, Tracey Rudnick, Pierre Ruhe, Ed Schneider and Jackie Mitchell, Mark Schuyler, Gene Seymour, Ken Shain, Jeffrey Sherman, Rita Sherman, Michael Shore, Chuck and Betsy Sigman, Holly and Eddie Silva, Phyllis Singer, Peter Skolnik, Maggie Smith, Patrick J. and Elizabeth Smith, Alan Stein, M. George Stevenson, Natalie Synhaivsky, Barbara and Conover Talbot, Terry and Hilary Dyson Teachout, Sandy Tolan, Anthony Tommasini and Ben McCommon, Carol Warstler, Alan Weeks and Pamela Rice, Henry Weil, Judith Weinraub, Keith Westerfield, Michael Windsor, Nora Wright, and Michael Zubal.

In memoriam: Leonard Altman, Tanash Atoynatan, Jeanne Batten, Andre Bernard, Kevin Brayne, Lee Buckley, Mary Jean Callahan, Kevin Cawley, Dean Henry Cook, Ralph Burk Dawson, Salvador Fernandez, G. Christopher Fish, Glenn Gould, Katharine Graham, Wallace Gray, Harry M. Hannah, Nancy Hitchings, Stephen Hodovan, Charles Jones, Vivian King, Kate Lamson, Otto Luening, Joseph McLellan, Robert "Bucky" Nichols, Jeffrey Ossen, Frank

Homer and Dorothy Batten Page, Ellis and Elizabeth Thaxton Page, Robert Z. and Esther Page, Jordan M. Phillips, Alan Rappaport, Bryan Robertson, Morton Schwimmer, Jack Sherman, Laura Singer, Ilse Singsen, R. W. Stallman, Gloria A. Sterry, Taylor Storer, Robert C. and Elizabeth L. Thaxton, Virgil Thomson, Hans Vonk, Jon H. Wetherell, Michael Wilcox, Rosalind Baker Wilson, Ed Wong, Henry Wong, and Irene Worth.

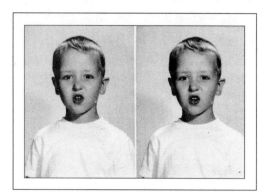